The Dead

By
Gare Allen

Also By Gare Allen
Available on Amazon.com

The 7 Novellas Series by Gare Allen

Book One- 7 Sessions

Book Two- 7 Regressions

Book Three- 7 Apparitions

Book Four- 7 Abductions

Book Five- 7 Projections

Book Six- 7 Predictions

Book Seven- 7 Reflections

The Dead: A True Paranormal Story. Copyright 2015 by Gare Allen. All rights reserved. No part of this book may be used or reproduced in any manner without written permission from the author. This is a true story; however some of the names have been changed or omitted. Any resemblances to actual places, people (living or dead), or incidents that happened that are not listed are purely coincidental. Prior written approval has been obtained from all parties who are mentioned in this book.

Preface

I've often been asked if the paranormal activities described in my short stories actually happened to me. My response has always been an honest one.

The stories are all based on actual events or at least what I perceived as real.

If you read the stories, you will see that the main character, Greer, doesn't blindly accept his experiences as real. He investigates them and allows them their due consideration before making a determination. He is more interested in what the events can do to enhance his existence and most importantly, his relationship with Ashley. Whether he accepts the abductions, incarnations, apparitions and projections as reality is really not all that important, as long as he learns from the experiences and grows.

This book explains my early interest and investigation into metaphysical teachings and is also an account of the spiritual and paranormal events that have occurred in my life, thus far.

Chapter One

I was twelve years old when my bed levitated itself.

It was close to ten o'clock on a school night when I decided to go to sleep and was immediately joined by the family dog, Patches.

While attending an elementary school carnival roughly five years earlier, my mother happened upon a box marked "Free Puppies." Inside remained the runt of the litter; small, covered in fleas and with various colored markings, hence the name, Patches. Mom immediately took pity on the pup and we brought her home. From that point forward, the small, mixed-breed dog's quality of life would, dramatically, increase.

As usual, she found a spot at the foot of the bed and curled into a ball.

My bedroom was located at the top of the mauve, shag carpeted stairs.

It was the early 1980's so don't judge.

Mine was the first bedroom at the beginning of a hallway that led to all the other sleep rooms.

I've never fallen asleep quickly, so I was wide awake a few minutes later when the bed suddenly elevated a few inches off the floor.

While suspended in mid-air, it wobbled slightly. I froze in terror, and the next few seconds felt more like minutes. Feelings of severe angst and confusion consumed me. It was similar to when you fly in a plane or take a ride on a roller coaster. It was a helpless sensation, but there weren't any safety mechanisms in place, and this wasn't a carnival ride. I could see Patches lift her head, prompted by the elevated and unstable motion.

After hovering for two to three seconds, the bed dropped hard and fast, back down to the floor. Patches jumped up and yelped a short, startled cry. My limbs shifted on their own, which provided me proof of my recent movement. Desperate to understand the obvious infraction of physics law, my mind frantically searched for a rational explanation. Simultaneously, I worked to hold back a panic attack by taking in deep breaths and slowly exhaling.

As if on cue, my older brother appeared in my open doorway. Having just walked up the stairs on his way to his bedroom, he stopped and asked, "What was that noise?"

Unable to collect my thoughts and formulate a response, while still trying to regulate my breathing, I simply looked at him. I imagined that my eyes were wide open. I must have had a mixture of confusion, disbelief and fright expressed on my face.

Growing up, I think most big brothers find their younger siblings strange and mostly uninteresting. I'm confident his perception was no exception. A look of wide-eyed terror would simply be another "weird little brother" moment and hardly worth the effort of investigation. He flashed me an eye roll, and then disappeared down the hallway. In hindsight, it was doubtful that he would have believed that the thud he heard as he climbed the stairs was actually my bed landing on the floor.

In shock, I remained motionless for another few minutes until the majority of my panic subsided and I finally found the courage to move. I sat up and looked around my small room.

The silence was eerie as I scanned the room for anything out of the ordinary. The closet door was open, and nothing but a filing cabinet and shoes looked back at me. Continuing my investigation, I confirmed that the window remained shut and was locked. That left just one obvious place to look: under the bed.

I leaned over the side of the mattress and allowed my head to hang down so that my view of the small space between the bed frame and the floor was upside down.

The light coming in from the open door provided just enough illumination to see through the dark space. I ran my hand along the carpet. It was cold. One more swipe of my extended arm resulted in my fingertips brushing against a soft piece of fabric. Assuming it was the match to one of my many, lonely socks, I pulled it out from underneath the bed.

I've always had a thing for, what I now refer to as, classic rock: The Beatles, The Who, The Rolling Stones, The Monkees, etc.

A close second musical favorite was heavy metal, in particular, AC/DC, Black Sabbath and Ozzy Osbourne.

Previously, my parents had reluctantly purchased an Ozzy tapestry and fulfilled my Christmas gift request. The tapestry was nothing more than a large handkerchief, adorned with images of Ozzy and his album covers. I would later see them at fairs and carnivals and understand that they were homemade, silkscreened products.

I held the square piece of fabric with both hands and sat up on the edge of my bed. My eyes inspected the tapestry as if I was going to see something on it that I hadn't before. The hallway light streaming through the door was no longer sufficient for my intense scrutiny, so I stood up, took a few steps toward the switch and flipped on the light. The instant illumination filled the room and I gasped at the edges of the kerchief. Each corner displayed an identical tack hole. Remembering that it had been hanging on my pre-teen wall, adjacent to soccer and football posters, I looked at the area above my bed.

Kids have the luxury of still believing in magic, Santa and in my case, a consistent, winning Tampa Bay Buccaneers team. Perhaps it was this naivety that kept me from sprinting from the room, as I stared at the four tacks on the wall that once held up the tapestry.

Nope, there weren't any tears in the corners of the handkerchief. It clearly hadn't been pulled down and I couldn't determine how it found its way off of my wall with the tacks remaining in place, only to be discovered beneath my bed.

After pulling the thumb tacks from the wall, I hung my Ozzy "artwork" back in place. My careful placement utilized the same tack holes in a concerted effort to deter the inevitable rants of my father regarding the insurmountable damage that tacks and push-pins inflict on wood paneling.

Yes, wood paneling. Again... 1980's.

Later, in early adulthood as I studied metaphysics, I would recall the specific images on the kerchief. Hazy and, most likely, unlicensed pictures of Ozzy in concert that were undoubtedly taken from magazines, adorned the corners, with random upside-down crosses filling the outer ring. The center boasted a large star that I would later understand to be a pentagram.

For those wondering, the juxtaposition of a satanic bandana as a Christmas present is not lost on me.

The frightening occurrence of my levitating bed opened my mind enough to allow an exploration of metaphysical concepts. In turn, those experiences would provide the storyline for my series of supernatural short stories, *The 7 Novellas Series.*

Chapter Two

There was an alignment of events that occurred when I was twenty-five that allowed me to investigate the non-secular nature of metaphysics, full time.

By "alignment of events", I mean that I left my job and took nine months off.

Suffice to say that I didn't like my job. I felt like I was stagnant, not challenged and all the other rationalizations that support leaving a job to "find yourself" and I felt like I actually did. At least, the self I was in my mid-twenties.

A day into my sabbatical, I was driving, without purpose or intent, and noticed a metaphysical bookstore. At first, I was hesitant, but where "twenty-something Gare" was concerned, curiosity ultimately called the shots, so I turned into the parking lot.

For the record, "forty-something Gare" is also curiosity's bitch.

While I didn't know it at the time, it was a "typical" new-age bookstore, evident by the glass angel figurines that I saw showcased in the windows as I approached the store front.

I was immediately hit with the formidable aroma of sandalwood incense when I entered. Countless books were categorized on generic brown shelves on various spiritual subjects, and soft, harp music played overhead as I browsed.

Harp music? Gare-one. Curiosity-zero.

My initial discomfort with the store's contents and atmosphere quickly waned when, after browsing the shelves, my fingers pulled out a book on reincarnation that was titled, *Many Lives, Many Masters* by Brian Weiss, MD.

I chose a book on past lives because I had an unexplainable interest in the subject that I had never satiated. I would later discover that my intrigue with the subject was actually fueled by my dreams.

This particular book was written by a doctor and, to my logical mind anyway, that made it credible. He presented the actual regression transcripts of one of his patients and her, often parallel, personal life circumstances. Dr. Weiss refrained from drawing conclusions and allowed the sessions to speak for themselves. The format allowed the reader to form their own opinions and arrive at their own determinations.

Sold.

I went to the counter and purchased my first spiritual book. The owner of the shop was working the counter and informed me that their monthly psychic fair would be taking place the following weekend. Readings were fifteen dollars for fifteen minutes and while it was *first come, first serve*, she recommended that I make an appointment. The day delivered another first as I paid for a psychic reading.

She then pointed to a list of unfamiliar names on a chalkboard and told me to pick the reader that I would like. For no conscious reason, I chose Dane.

I went home and devoured the book on reincarnation in one sitting. The possibility of living multiple lives truly intrigued me. Moreover, the process of light hypnosis regression to uncover the events of previous lifetimes all but blew my mind.

Good or bad, I am my father's son and everything must pass through my left-brain, analytical filter. I returned to the bookstore countless times and read every book I could find on the subject until research was no longer sufficient. I needed to apply my findings, and I did.

While reincarnation was the bait that lured me into metaphysical study, it was my first psychic reading and subsequent friendship with Dane that set the hook.

Saturday arrived and I drove to the bookstore early, excited about my reading. I browsed through more books and wandered through the attending crowd as I waited for my scheduled divination.

I caught bits and pieces of the conversations as I passed by the attendees. Some were newbies, like me, who were preparing their questions for the psychics. Others were self-proclaimed ascended beings who were there for a slight alignment of their chakras to weather their recent bleak, astrological forecast and Mercury's unfortunate status in retrograde.

Yeah, I thought the same thing.

Eventually, I was called into a large room that was normally used for spiritual classes. Readers sat at individual card tables that were spaced thirty feet apart to provide the illusion of privacy. As I eavesdropped on the conversations that began between the readers and the customers, I quickly categorized them.

Some were returning customers who received weekly readings to determine the best course of action with regard to their financial and emotional well-being.

Others were first-timers and were there because their lives had experienced an unanticipated change and were truly unsure of how to proceed.

Overall, they were normal looking, average men and women of all ages with a common hope of receiving some guidance.

Eventually, I was introduced to Dane. He stood five feet and ten inches high with dark hair and a thin, black mustache. I later learned that he was of Spanish descent.

I sat down across from him and he handed me a stack of playing cards.

"Shuffle the cards and concentrate on your question," he told me.

I took a quick glance around the room and noted that some of the readers opted for traditional palm readings while others received prophecy through the use of Tarot cards.

"You use regular playing cards?" I asked.

His eyes remained mostly patient as his well-rehearsed explanation began. "It's called Cartomancy. My grandmother taught me when I was very young. I prefer them to

The Tarot as they can provide more specific information."

My expression must have told him that I had no follow-up questions. "Shuffle the cards and focus on your question."

Given the fifteen-minute timeframe, I decided to ask for insight on two subjects: a new job and a relationship, since I was currently unemployed and unattached.

I shuffled and focused on employment. I gave him back the stack, and he spread the cards across the table. He then asked me to choose ten cards. Randomly, I pulled the cards aside, and he placed them on the table in a pyramid-type layout.

I noticed that the majority of the cards were hearts and diamonds. My delivery was confident as I applied the, admittedly simple, concept of jumper cables. "Red is positive and black is negative?"

Dane smiled. "In a sense, yes. The cards show us where the energy of a situation is headed. If the direction is desired, then in that sense, it is positive or good. If not, then we can make changes. It may not be negative, just headed down a different road. Does that make sense?"

Sugar coated, but accepted. "Yup."

Dane read through the cards regarding employment. Impressively, he described my past work experience in detail and eventually prophesized that when I had returned to my home, I would find a message on my answering machine from an interested company to whom I had applied.

I shuffled the cards again, this time focusing on a romantic relationship. He used the same card layout, except this time, every card was black.

"Well, that can't be good." I determined.

I truly believe he tried, but couldn't hold back a chuckle as he reviewed the spades and clubs. He carefully and compassionately told me that he did not see a relationship in the near future. It simply wasn't, "in the cards."

After thanking him for the reading, I returned home, where I listened to a message on my answering machine from an interested company, asking for an interview.

While I had no reason to suspect Dane of any kind of foul play and despite my own experiences, it would have been naïve of me to fully accept the existence of psychic abilities after only one reading.

I would have many more readings from Dane and other psychics over the years. Many would provide intimate knowledge of my life and predictions that would unfold as they described. They gave me unwavering proof of their abilities which reminded me of a few previously forgotten, prophetic experiences of my own.

When I was fifteen, my father, two brothers and me were standing in a circle and engaged in conversation in our large kitchen. As my oldest brother was speaking, I looked at his hand that was holding a large, glass of water. While he appeared to have a firm grip on it, I knew that he would be dropping it soon. I cannot explain how or why I knew this, but I did. For a minute or so I waited for what I was sure to happen. And it did.

As the glass fell I reached down and caught it before it fell to the laminate kitchen floor.

Witnessing my reaction, my dad and siblings stared at me in disbelief. My father, with an incredulous look, said, "Nice reflexes."

I didn't bother explaining my premonition.

Another instance occurred when I was working an unholy five a.m. shift at work. Shortly after the hour, I was standing with a small group of co-workers around the break room table. They were searching through the boxes of donuts for their particular favorite.

One of the clerical women was approaching, having descended from the upstairs office. Although I had never interacted or even spoken to her, I clearly "saw" her, in my mind's eye, asking for a jelly donut. Furthermore, she would explain that they had been her favorite as a kid and hadn't had one in many years.

I decided to test my prophetic abilities. I turned to another co-worker, Pete, who was standing next me and told him exactly what she was going to say.

The woman arrived to the table and recited the words I had heard them in my mind, verbatim.

Pete's jaw dropped and he stared at me, but never said anything.

Through my readings, it would become clear that those that possess the gift of divination can only do so if the client is open to the process.

I wasn't always an open person and certainly didn't wear my heart on my sleeve. I allowed others "in" on a case by case basis and allowed "full access entry" to only a few. Unfortunately, being "closed off" would sometimes create a barrier to those trying to read my energy and provide insight.

Likening this to a state of imbalance only fueled my desire to expand my mind and spirituality through the continued investigation of metaphysics.

Chapter Three

I learned that Dane was not only a reader but the Assistant Manager at the bookstore. My frequent visits fostered a friendship that prompted him to invite me over to his place for a channeling session.

My curiosity won another round. Surprisingly, I found myself completely at ease and receptive to…well, whatever a channeling session was.

We hung out and chatted for a while. After devouring New York style pizza and a few beers Dane, curiously, lowered the thermostat setting in an already cold room and then sat on the floor of his living room with his legs crossed. I was on the other side of the room, completely unaware of what I was about to witness, despite his explanation.

"I'm going to channel my spirit guide for you."

I had no idea what to expect but I asked, "Should I move closer so I can hear you better?"

He chuckled. "Don't worry, you'll hear her."

"Her?" I thought to myself.

Dane took a series of deep breaths. Those were followed by a humming that gradually increased, not only in volume, but also in vibration. I could feel his hum resonate through my body. After a few moments the throaty sound became a voice; a woman's voice.

I've met women with deep voices and men with high voices, but their voices were their own. Suddenly, Dane's voice was gone and replaced with that of a female who delivered a loud, exaggerated and enunciated message.

"We are pleased to speak with you," she said.

I watched, mesmerized, as Dane appeared to be in some kind of trance. His head slowly rotated on his neck, and his eyelids shuttered slightly, yet remained closed. The room was palpable with a warm, oddly embracing, energy. As a result, the temperature dramatically increased during the thirty-minute session.

Now I understand why he lowered the temperature on the thermostat.

For a moment, I scrutinized Dane and fully expected him to break from his performance so we could both share a laugh. But, he didn't. His body remained still as his head slowly moved from the left and to the right in a consistent, smooth manner. The female's voice boomed out of him, making it imminently clear that I was speaking to someone other than Dane.

While my mind quickly accepted the idea of channeling a spirit, it also cautioned the possibility of demon possession.

At the mere consideration, she addressed my concern and explained the mutual agreement between her and Dane.

"There is an arrangement with the vehicle which allows us to speak through him."

"Vehicle?" I kept my thoughts to myself, for now.

As each consecutive question entered my mind, she answered it, before I could ask it, audibly.

"Indeed." She paused and Dane's head shook slightly before it resumed the smooth movement from left to right. It was here that I would witness her sense of humor as well as her ability to experience annoyance. "His intake of the carbonated beverage makes it difficult to maintain a connection."

"I'll tell him to lay off the beers." I quipped, in my head.

"He knows." She responded, playfully.

She went on to explain her role as a spirit guide. Yes, they are here to help us. And yes, they will send us signs to assist us so that we remain on the chosen path.

"Chosen path? Chosen by whom?" I wondered to myself.

She explained. "You arrive into the physical world with a personal mission. The particulars are known to your subconscious, which is where your spirit, or soul, resides and works closely with emotion. Hence, your gut instincts, intuition, etc."

She paused and I wondered if I should have been taking notes.

"Front and center on the physical platform, is the ego. Ego has its own ever-changing agenda and needs, which may or may not coincide with the original marching orders of your soul. This is where guides, or angels, step in to help you discern needs from wants."

I had often struggled with the challenges of always doing what I *felt* was right rather than what I *thought* was the correct action. I didn't always have a *feeling* regarding a specific decision.

For example, should I take a promotion or not? My mind says to take the promotion and the increase in salary, but I don't have an emotional resonance to the choice aside from ego's opportunity to brag to someone about it. However, it would seem beneficial to take the elevation in status and compensation. So, there has to be a balance of what we want versus what we need, coupled with what is best for us or what is intended for us in our lifetime.

Second, how do I decipher what is a message from my inner self, so to speak, and what is the direction from my ego or personality? It's not like one of them has a noticeable accent to help me differentiate between the two. Sure, I often have strong feelings that seem to emanate from beneath ego's surface, but those don't always serve, what I view as, my best interest or needs.

Pulling on my years of management experience, I determined a shorter, time-saving, route to understanding and results: simply tell me what my specific life plan happens to be.

To my dismay, the disembodied spirit withheld the requested information in favor of not-so-frivolous things such as free will, individual growth and most importantly, karma.

Characteristically anticipating my next question, she explained that spirit connects with us directly through our dreams. The ever present caveat being that the language of our subconscious is symbols. "We speak to you through your dreams. Look to them for guidance"

"The content of my dreams rival any narcotic-induced hallucination and makes as much sense." I thought to myself.

"Perhaps an example would be of assistance in your understanding." She offered.

Cleverly, she referenced a dream of mine from a previous night's sleep that was known only to me. After describing my dream to me, in detail, I sat stunned, quiet and motionless.

In the dream, I was standing in an open field. Strangely, I had complete control of the elements. First, I would summon fire with the dramatic hand motion similar to lifting something from the ground. Then, I would raise my arms and motion heavy rain down to extinguish the flames. This was followed by a swirl of my arms above my head that brought gusts of wind that lifted debris from the ground to be sucked into funnels of vacuumed air. The "dream me" commanded the elementals with ease and flair repeatedly, until I awoke.

If this entire session was some kind of elaborate parlor trick, then I was thoroughly impressed. I hadn't told anyone about my dream, and, as was often the case where my dreams were concerned, I recalled it in vivid detail. Also, the content seemed to lend itself nicely to her subsequent explanation of dream content and my recent interests.

I found my voice. "How could you possibly know about my dream?" I asked the spirit of the disembodied woman who was speaking through a man.

Clearly, my normal days were behind me.

With her consistently loud and clear tone, she explained, "The events were not a dream; they were memories."

I was back to stunned, quiet and motionless.

She continued. "You recalled a memory of a previous incarnation. One, in which, you were a Shaman who had learned control of fire, wind and rain. Your recent study of reincarnation and the desire to uncover your past lives had reached your subconscious and it fulfilled your request."

"So, memories of this lifetime are stored in the brain but those of past lives are kept filed in the subconscious?" I asked, silently proud of my early understanding.

While my comprehension was extremely superficial, she felt it served at least the initial introduction of the subject matter. Dane's spirit guide confirmed my assertion with what would become her trademark response during our future sessions. "Indeed."

Now that she had my trust, understanding and what would become an insatiable hunger for more meta-teachings, she chose to close her presentation with the umbrella principle of metaphysics; we create our own reality.

This concept elicits one of two responses. The first is a pure joy that we have the ability to create the desired particulars of our existence. The second is that we must assume full responsibility for our lives and everything that happens, for we create all of it.

I can tell you, from experience, that the former is much more pleasant.

I would find that in order to fully allow the subconscious to play out the specific life experiences from my spiritual blueprint, my ego would need to be kept in check.

That has yet to happen.

Thus began an ongoing struggle between ego and spirit within me. My ego, partnered with the left side of my brain, knows best because it is practical. Or, my spirit, aligned with my emotions, knows best because it has divine information and insight. Sometimes the two would align in a rare agreement of a course of action that fostered a sense of balance; only to be short lived until the next life decision presented itself.

I needed more insight and understanding of how to navigate, beneficially, through physical reality. To this, she opened the door for self-exploration.

"Within your subconscious are your dreams, desires, wants and self-worth. Alternately, it houses your doubts, fears, guilt and insecurities. As you live your daily life, in this particular incarnation, think of your subconscious as a garden. The desire to create something in your physical world plants a seed in your garden. Be careful to care and nourish the seeds of desire with love and positivity so that they grow and flourish. When you fail to manifest that which you desire, you may look to your fears and feelings of deservability. In this analogy of a garden, they would be the weeds that choke the new plantings."

With that, I reconsidered my definition of the term, "soul-searching".

Dane's head began to jerk from its smooth movements and he opened his eyes. Having returned from, wherever the hell he went, he looked at me and quickly grounded himself back into his surroundings as he asked, "Did she come through?"

Surprised, I asked a question in response. "You don't have any memory of the last thirty minutes?"

He was visibly hot and sweating, despite the chilling air blasting from the vents.

I recall that after one session, Dane was so hot that he repeatedly ran up and down his stairs to release the intense energy.

"No, I'm not conscious when she comes through." He then wiped the moisture from his forehead with his hand. "So, what did she say?"

I relayed the content of the session to him and he was genuinely pleased that I found it helpful.

I left his home with a mixture of feelings. I was riveted by the new experience yet strangely comforted by it as well. She had knowledge of my dreams but I didn't feel violated. If anything, she helped me understand them better and, for that, I was grateful.

I would have many more sessions over the coming months. Regardless of whether or not I believed it was actually unconscious channeling, I had the choice and opportunity to explore the ideas and perspectives.

I would need proof before I declared my belief. So, I dove, head first, into the concept of reincarnation.

Chapter Four

Consideration of the concepts was only half a meal and I needed "practical" applications. With the purchase of a past-life regression cassette, I set out on a nightly quest to uncover my previous incarnations.

For those of you born this side of the millennium, a cassette was a plastic, audio device that was popular after vinyl yet before compact discs. It was the taller, better looking brother of the eight-track tape. For additional information, I recommend you Google, "outdated technology".

Every night for weeks, I used the cassette. The tape guided me through a relaxation technique where I relaxed my toes, my legs and then every part of my body; working my way to the top of my head.

The next step was to breathe in through my nose to the count of six and out through my mouth at the same duration while disregarding any intrusive thoughts. The woman on the cassette instructed me to visualize a ship on the ocean and move it toward the horizon where it would find a previous lifetime. Then, the images appeared in my mind.

The first life I connected to was, in linear terms, the most recent. I learned of a relatively short incarnation in Chicago, Illinois in which I was born in early October of 1935 and died in late December of 1968.

An interesting aside is that I was born January 12, 1969. My mother had told me that my due date was the middle of December. In an effort to allow everyone the enjoyment of the holiday outside of a hospital, they induced labor several days before Christmas. But, I would not emerge until almost two weeks into January, at an inconvenient 3:45 a.m.

Over several regression sessions I recalled key events of my previous life in Chicago that occurred during a three month period of March through June of 1958. Unlike the telling of this lifetime in my first short story, *7 Sessions*, I did not "see" the events chronologically.

In my very first regression I experienced a horrific motorcycle accident. I saw myself, in 1958, in downtown Chicago. I was driving a motorcycle with a woman on the back of the seat with her arms wrapped my waist. I had dark hair and eyes, a square chin and a rugged, sun weathered face. My black leather jacket was blindingly shiny under the summer sun. Somehow, I knew my name to be Charles.

Behind Charles was a beautiful, blond-haired woman who rested her face on his wide back. She wore a pink scarf, which blew behind her as they rode through the downtown streets. I knew that her name was Julia.

The next scene I saw in my mind's eye brought tears to my real ones.

Charles noticed a small patch of oil or water on the pavement. He couldn't tell which one it was. He managed to avoid the spill only to land the front tire in a deep pothole. The bike bounced out of the hole and the back wheel came off the ground and threw Charles off the cycle.

He landed on his back with a hard thud. With the bike still in view and, to his horror, the accident before him was far from over. In a nightmare beyond description, he witnessed his beautiful Julia being dragged under the motorcycle as it continued down the damaged road.

Her scarf was entwined in the back tire spokes. As her soft face was scraped off by the hot asphalt, she desperately called out for help. Charles could barely hear her pleas, and later would wish he hadn't. He endured the maddening sound of metal clanking and scratching as the bike began to slow.

The bike stopped after another sixty feet and fell silent of the once thriving motor and horrific screams. A resulting display of a motionless haunting pile of twisted metal and rubber covering a lifeless beauty was the image now engrained in Charles' mind.

Charles could not feel his legs. He screamed for Julia but she did not reply. He cried out one more time, "Julia!"

So, my first past life regression was somewhat light on the cheeriness. But, the brochure did promise that I would witness "key events" and that seemed quite significant, if not conclusive.

Through another regression I would uncover the unsettling outcome of the accident to be Charles' disability and overwhelming guilt. His legs paralyzed, he would spend the next eleven years in a wheelchair; miserable and blaming himself for the death of his girlfriend.

Another aside is that up until this point I had never been able to sleep with a sheet or comforter on my legs. I would cover my torso but leave the bottom half exposed. If I were to cover my legs, I would begin to panic as if I were claustrophobic. After this regression, and still today, I am able to pull the covers over my entire body without any issue.

The dark content of this past incarnation notwithstanding, I was excited to have successfully uncovered the specifics and called Dane to share them with him.

I was not prepared for the level of confirmation that I would receive regarding my memories and found that he had the same recall, but from the perspective of Julia.

My left brain skepticism dictated that I allow him to relay his findings to me first, thus proving to me that his recall of the events that mirrored mine, were indeed, real.

The parallels were undeniable.

Dane recalled that Julia worked in her grandmother's bar while I remembered that Charles met her in that bar.

Initially insignificant, he described Julia's cat including color and gender. I had seen her cat during my regressions as well. Often it would jump up and down on a brown couch while Charles and Julia talked.

Dane gave me specifics about Charles. "I never saw him without a black, leather jacket. When he wasn't riding his motorcycle, he was working on it."

The clincher was that he had intimate knowledge of their fateful accident and I cringed at his words.

"I felt the hot cement against my face. The scarf was caught in the wheel and I was dragged."

Thus, I was convinced that there was something to this "stuff". I continued to use the tape and uncovered several more lifetimes and would tell their stories in *7 Regressions*.

Hungry for more of my past life resume, I used every quiet evening available to continue my regressions. While they yielded memories of more incarnations, I was lucky enough to be regressed by an experienced, past life expert.

Having used a gift certificate that was given to me by a friend on my birthday, I regressed to a life as a captured prisoner in the French Army who was held in an underground prison with several other men.

For days, I sat in my own urine and feces as my wounds, inflicted by the soldiers, festered with infection. As the men died off in the subterranean cell, the stench of sickness and death burned my nose.

Becoming delirious from the lack of food and water, I imagined myself back in my small, home town in France. My days had been spent working odd jobs for quick money while my nights were spent drinking away the hard earned coins at a tavern.

A desire for stability in my life fueled my decision to join the military.

It took twelve long, excruciating days before my body surrendered to death at the hands of starvation, dehydration and sickness.

In an equally sad lifetime, I recalled being a young kitchen wench. As a child, I was taken from my sleep and transported in the bottom of a slave boat to the island of Saint Kitts in the West Indies.

Working in a sugar mill, I survived by keeping to myself and working hard and in silence. It was easy to determine what the guards would tolerate and what they wouldn't as they beat a child almost hourly and announced their infraction of their rules.

One day, one of the men noticed my behaved demeanor and took me home as a gift to his wife.

In a different, albeit nicer, prison, but still enslaved, I worked day and night and answered to "Girl", as they never bothered to ask my name. I cooked and cleaned from early morning until late at night for more than eight years. Alone and ignored during my last days, I died, unloved, at the very young age of twenty and was tossed in a public grave.

Dane also shared with me his recollection of another shared lifetime in very ancient Egypt. It would take years to uncover many of the specifics of the complicated existence. Even today, I don't fully know the outcome of that incarnation.

What I do recall, is a very lonely existence as a Pharoah.

Yes, I know, everyone thinks they were royalty in a past life. But, this one is different.

My name was Merkharu and I was born from a human mother but seeded by an extraterrestrial father. After many sessions I would recall much of the incarnation and feature this lifetime prominently in the short story, *7 Abductions*.

During my regression, I witnessed the landing of a spaceship on the sands of ancient Egypt. The people were frightened as bright, shiny objects descended from the sky. Their landing, while eerily quiet, was overshadowed by the emergence of very tall humanoid creatures. Physically the differences were minor and the awe at the sight of their flying crafts soon waned as they struggled to comprehend their ability to communicate with their minds rather than their mouths.

The visitors allowed the indigenous crowd to find the courage to approach them. After some time they did just that and their fear began to subside. Soon their presence became commonplace.

Over time, the aliens offered insight to the use of gems and crystals and eventually pyramid power. They used the power of their minds to move rock into place creating immense structures that were astrologically aligned and tapped into a cosmic magic that is now lost to the changed constellations in the sky.

Their mission seemed one of universal philanthropy. Having won the people's trust, they began to copulate with the Egyptian woman. Merkharu was the first of eight of his kind. A half-breed, revered as a miracle to the Egyptian people and a success to the aliens despite his loss of height due to the union of physiology.

Twenty-four years after his birth he ruled the people of ancient Egypt. True earth Egyptians worked as slaves while the seven born half-breeds practiced magic as priests and developed rituals and spells that would be used for centuries.

The aliens left Earth with clear instruction for Merkharu to procreate with female half breeds to continue the new line of the more intelligent, capable human. His offspring were only one quarter alien but the abilities were in the DNA which was the very goal of the now departed visitors.

His specific agenda dictated Merkharu's actions for another fifteen years until his human frailty allowed a dental infection that traveled to his heart and eventually took his life. He left behind countless children that he never knew, having lived life on Earth void of the human experience of a family unit.

My lifetime was tasked with the daily responsibility of merging my alien DNA with the human beings. I "worked" tirelessly at the endeavor.

Not a terrible lifetime…

Dane was never willing to divulge much of his memory of this shared incarnation, but I did know his name to be Kapherus.

Some, rather, most will declare my regressions as simply my imagination. It's actually the opposite for me as my creativity stems from my experiences. Also, my confirmation of a shared life with Dane supports my trust in the validity of my memories. But, despite what others may think, I was, and remain, a grounded individual.

There was a theme building among my trips down past life memory lane. In each, I was alone which helped me make some correlations between the past personalities and myself in my twenties.

The time spent alone in the past could very well have shaped my current, antisocial attitude. While I forced myself to participate in activities and socialize with others, I've always been quite content while being home alone.

In fact, even today, I despise large gatherings. Trade shows, conventions, and the like take their toll on me after the first day or two. I despise being herded around like cattle from meeting rooms to social halls. The heavy amounts of mass produced, convention food that is served three times a day could easily induce a carbohydrate coma. Coffee and other caffeinated drinks are then consumed to counter the sleep-inducing effects over-eating and the daily cycle continues for the duration of the often, week-long event.

As you can guess, I am not one to be part of the crowd and follow the masses. Since you are reading this book, I'll assume that you are not dissimilar and also prefer to dance to your own mix tape.

The lives of servitude also had an interesting effect. While I don't have an issue being told what to do by a superior, I take great exception to not being told *exactly* what to do. That is, provide me with specific direction with every bit of detail possible.

My attitude is fueled in part by the lifetime as the young, slave girl who learned to avoid beatings by working hard and performing her tasks perfectly and as expected.

Further reinforcement of my trait stems from the time spent as soldier in an uber-structured French Army.

It's easy to say that my questionable behavior or personality quirks are a result of lifetimes of experience and I just have to live with it.

However, it's much more difficult to strive to understand why I am like I am, based on those previous experiences. It can be difficult to accept that those traits may not serve my best interest in the here and now and thus, work through and perhaps even release them.

For me, that's where the growth occurs. Changing a personality flaw from another lifetime is similar to changing a bad habit from childhood.

It doesn't matter if an unwanted personality trait, habit or attitude was created a year ago, ten years ago, fifty years ago or during the last incarnation. If it's there, it's there and I have chosen to deal with them.

Alternatively, the time alone in the previous lives has given me the strength to be self-sufficient and the confidence to pursue my own paths.

It seems to me that I have a debt to pay to my past personalities. They lived and sometimes suffered, to give me some of the beneficial qualities that I possess today. I choose to repay that debt by making use of those traits while creating new ones, for the next life.

Chapter Five

I shared my findings with my family and friends and opened the door for enduring and loving ridicule.

From time to time a small, handful of acquaintances would take me aside and ask me to tell them more about my experiences and then share with me their own. But, most kept their interest closeted for fear of character defamation.

Personally, I was, and still am, hardly concerned with other people's opinions.

I recall a co-worker asking me to explain the relaxation technique that I used to regress into past lives. We spent the better part of our lunch break discussing the potential results and he promised to share his experiences with me.

However, within the week, he would stand with another co-worker in verbal ridicule of my metaphysical endeavors and never admit his interest.

I was more annoyed than angry at him, but mostly, I felt sorry for him. If he didn't have the courage to investigate the things that called out to him, then how would he ever embrace his true passions in life?

After delving deep into my past lives, I accepted my teachings, ventured forward and began reading about astral projection. The very idea of being able to travel anywhere and -- unbelievably -- *anytime*, was even more exciting to me than uncovering my past lives.

The first book I read was Robert Monroe's *Journeys Out of the Body*. He described countless out-of-body experiences as his spirit left his physical body and possessed the ability to travel anywhere, via the astral plane, in an instant.

Through my reading I would understand that the astral plane mirrored the physical. The astral looked into the physical but the physical did not, by definition anyway, see into the astral.

Given the disembodied spirit's channeled messages and my half-alien past-life recall, this endeavor was already in my wheelhouse, so, I bought the cassette.

The process used basically the same relaxation technique found on the past life regression tape. However, once relaxed, you would "will" your "astral self" out of your physical body.

My early results came after I fell asleep. I would partially wake as I was lifting out and experience varied levels of control.

During my very first attempt I fell asleep during the relaxation process and then woke as I was lifting out. I floated up and my perspective was the surroundings of my bedroom. While I could plainly see my physical form sleeping on my bed, I could not see my *astral* body. Although I felt them, I was unable to see my hands or legs so I don't know what I was wearing or even if I still looked like me.

When I realized that I was "out", I thought, immediately, that I wanted to go to the moon. After a whirling sound around me, I felt a surge of rapid movement and then I was there.

Walking beside me on the lunar surface, as if completely normal, was a beautiful, dark haired woman. She boasted impossibly high cheek bones and large, dark, loving and knowing eyes. The angelic creature stood inside a glow of soft, white light. She seemed pleased at my presence and briefly described to me the art of astral travel.

"On the astral plane, your thoughts instantly create. Focus is necessary to maintain your location."

I felt a sense of achievement as we walked. Looking down from the surface of the moon to Earth, I could see a long, silver cord stretching from somewhere on my backside.

The woman explained its purpose. "It will remain tied to your body and connected until your physical death."

I then asked her name and I received this response, "I am your spirit guide, your protector and family. My name is Selene."

I woke with these images and the majority of our conversation fresh in my mind. I had taken to leaving my journal and a pen on my night stand so that I could document my dreams and, now, astral projections. I logged the details of the occurrence in my journal under a new chapter called, OBE's or out of body experiences.

My subsequent projections occurred often as I continued to use the cassette on a consistent basis; but only after I fell asleep.

During the relaxation process, I would choose my destination. As I lifted out, I would become conscious and aware and then immediately recall my travel plans.

On one occasion, I went to see my friend, Chad. I ended up in his living room where I observed his grandmother watching television. In an effort to obtain validation of the experience, I asked him about this the next day. Chad explained that his grandparent watched television every night and, unable to validate my presence, he discounted the event as a dream.

On another attempt, I chose to go to another friend's house but I made it as far as the top of my home and was unable to move. I just hung above the house and was, strangely able to view my surroundings, all

360 degrees, at once. Eventually, I went back into my body. It appeared that that particular destination was not accessible, although I never found out why.

Landing back into my physical body was always fast and resulted in my immediate awakening. I would be left with the residual sensation that I had fallen and landed on my bed.

Sometimes I would become conscious long after I had lifted out of my body and find myself in an unfamiliar location. I recall finding myself in a strange house and moving freely through the home of an unfamiliar family. As I drifted through their kitchen I felt as if I was invading their privacy. I could hear them speak but their language was not known to me.

I moved to the second level of their home where I saw two young boys playing. The younger one looked up and stared right into my eyes. He looked terrified and at the realization that he could see me, I "landed" back into my body and woke with my heart pounding.

I imagined a scared little boy telling his parents that he saw a ghost floating in the house and his access to scary movies restricted for the next several months.

Sorry, kid.

One day, Dane visited the house. During his stay, he sensed a dark energy in the corner of the living room and suggested that I use sage and white candles to remove it.

What I had yet to tell him was that the prior night I had left my body and immediately encountered Selene. She was standing in the doorway of my bedroom as I lifted out and pointed toward the corner of the living room. She told me, very clearly, "They should not be here."

Dane's indication of a negative energy helped me to make sense of Selene's astral message.

My insatiable curiosity tugged at my leash, and I attempted time-travel. Any temporal scientist worth his salt will attest that time, as it exists in physical reality, is subject to the laws of our physical world. Like anything else, it alters its state of being once outside of that world. The astral plane, insofar as we understand it, allows a manipulation of physical time. Thus, I decided to visit "Past Gare".

I performed my relaxation exercise and allowed an intense vibration to consume by body. As per usual, I fell asleep and then woke as I was lifting out and quickly recalled my desire to visit my most recent past life self.

Thanks to many entertaining time-travel movies, I assumed that I would see the events of that lifetime from the safe perspective of the "past me".

Unfortunately, that didn't happen.

What actually occurred was that I found myself flying toward a beautiful island. It was nighttime, but the water and lush landscape's beauty glistened in the bright moonlight. I landed and walked toward a blond woman that stood at the edge of the water. Unfortunately, I couldn't see her face so I moved closer and just before I reached her, she turned.

It was Julia and she was stunning. She smiled lovingly and her blue eyes shimmered as they reflected the moon's glow. I wasn't sure if she had passed and was now a ghost or I was truly back in the 1950's and she was on an island somewhere.

Before I could ask, I was attacked. A very angry Charles rushed toward me. Instantly recognizing him from my own regressions, I didn't expect him to be aggressive because…well, he was me. His charge sent me back to my physical body and left me with the distinct impression that he was protecting Julia.

Despite his assault, I was eager to return. I was growing frustrated that I only became partially aware of my projections after falling asleep. I wanted to lift out, while fully awake. I whined to Dane and he told me that my spirit guide had a message for me. "Selene will be assisting you in a fully conscious astral experience, very soon."

Soon was actually the very next night. As I began my usual relaxation exercise, I felt invisible fingers touch the bottom of my feet. Suddenly, a surge of intense vibration, stronger than I had ever experienced, resonated throughout my body. My head throbbed from the building pressure and I began consciously lifting out of my physical body.

Unprepared and scared, I willed myself back in. Within seconds, it was over and I had missed my chance to do what I complained that I had not been able to accomplish.

I called Dane the next morning, but he had already been told of my actions by his guide, which was further validation that it was a real event.

Selene made herself known to me on another occasion. I was taking an employment test in a large room with hundreds of other applicants. The testing was sectioned and timed and we were required to put our pencils down at the sound of the timer. It had been clearly explained that any violation of the rules surrounding our timed responses would disqualify our potential employment.

During one of the sections I had only one more question to answer and knew the answer but the timer had sounded and the facilitator had instructed us to put down our writing tools. I considered the risk of very quickly bubbling in the circle. In the same instant, I put down my number two writing tool at the direction of Selene.

I heard and felt, in my ear, the words, "Put it down."

Her hot breath and the vibration of her voice were all characteristics of a corporeal person whispering into my ear. I jerked around expecting to see one of the wandering monitors with a pointed, scolding finger aimed directly at me. There was no one was within four feet of me.

A few heads leered at me in response to my sudden movement but they quickly lost interest in me and resumed their focus on the continued testing.

Later after the tests were over, I went home and immediately called Dane. He answered my call with "I heard you made direct contact with Selene today."

I was floored, but in a good way. The more I experienced of the spirit world, the more I craved it.

After getting a "B+" in *"Connecting with Your Spirit Guide"*, I resumed my focus on astral projection.

At this point my past life regressions had provided a good look into my rearview mirror so I focused on the concept of meeting, "Future Gare". That, disappointingly, did not occur. Instead, I visited several different realities of Earth's future.

In one, it was well into the thirtieth century and the planet had been reborn. It was lush and green and free of pollution and environmental degrade. I was met by a small group of future humans who, physically, appeared mostly unchanged from current-day homo-sapiens, but were pleasant, kind and overly affectionate.

I realize that their friendly demeanor should be seen as a positive thing but "twenty-first century Gare" prefers his fellow humans distant and outside of his personal space.

I had flown in over a vast, green field in what appeared to be a colorful, glorious spring day. Lush, vibrant colors adorned the edges of the wide expanse and provided a stunning background to the countless, active small animals and birds as they searched for food.

The future humans were smiling broadly and seemed generally excited to see me. Again, as was the case with Selene on the moon, I got the impression that my presence was a pleasing accomplishment.

I "landed" on the bright green grass in front of them. They formed a circle around me and a tall blond, male immediately filled in the thousand year gap for me. "The people of Earth all but destroyed themselves. From the ashes of destruction and near extinction, life eventually returned." He motioned toward his physical body lying not far from us and I understood that they were also, astral bodies. He continued. "We inhabit the planet in our astral form and use our physical bodies when necessary."

I felt a tug at my mid-section. The man smiled at me and said "Goodbye". After another tug, I woke up in my bed with the familiar sensation of having fallen. I then realized the reason for my rapid return to my physical body; I had to pee.

In another future, I was witness to literal, Hell on Earth. The veil between the world of the living and the world of the dead had broken down. Demons, ghosts and dark creatures terrorized the planet.

While I walked among them I could feel the dark, heavy energy of the evil beings behind me. I turned and they would be inches from my face.

Crawling across the ground were thousands of tiny brown, spiderlike creatures. They moved quickly, on eight legs, and their long antennas waved high above them as they moved across dead grass. Behaving like scavengers, the rapid moving bottom feeders picked the remains off of the skeletons of both humans and animals that were strewn across the brown, dead grounds.

Countless flying beasts swarmed the skies and blocked the sun's illumination, thus bringing darkness to the Earth. The black, aerial beings breathed fire like the mythical dragon but were more avian in appearance with their long beaks and sharp talons. Their high pitched screeches drowned out the sounds of whatever indigenous Earth animals remained.

I was never harmed or even touched. I assumed that it was because I was viewing the events from the astral plane. The humans residing on the physical plane struggled to keep them at a distance using salt, holy water and crosses. I received the impression that the merging of worlds was the result of alien involvement, but I was not aware of the reason.

Afterward, per the suggestion of Dane, I recorded the experience in a birthday gift that he had given to me; an Egyptian symbol adorned journal. Having used a computer for almost everything, I discovered that my penmanship is that of a three year old with a nervous twitch and quite illegible.

I chose to simply print the emails that I would send to Dane which described my encounters and place them, folded, inside the journal.

As I type this, the stack of emails sits to my left, still inside the Egyptian journal. Reading through them, it's clear that my astral travels were a mission of meta-self-discovery. Thankfully, I had them to review while writing *7 Projections*.

I finally made some sense of something that I still recall from when I was around the age of seven. I woke up one morning and joined my family in the living room. To this day, I can still remember the dream I was about to describe to my father.

I was flying above a road, at night, while watching a full grown, male lion run alongside me. Even in the dark, the monster cat was vivid and I could sense its fear as it appeared to run away from something.

My father was watching television and before I could share my dream, I heard him shout to my mother in the other room that, overnight, a lion had escaped from Busch Gardens. The news reported that the zoo workers had been trying to capture the giant cat during the night and for most of the morning.

Today, I truly believe that I had astral projected and found myself beside the escaped lion.

As a child I would often wake from my dreams and nightmares with a strong, residual emotional attachment. Perhaps that is the reason I have been able to remember them in such vivid detail.

I can recall a childhood, recurring dream where our pool room was filled with various monsters. I saw, among others, mummies, ghosts, Frankenstein and werewolves. My mother told me that I had better get back to bed because at the stroke of midnight, the vampire would awaken. I looked over at the gathering of monsters and one of the werewolves began chasing me back to my bedroom. During every occurrence of this dream, this is where I would wake up.

On the night of the final nightmare, I awoke and heard leaves crunching beneath what I assumed were feet outside of my window. Our yard boasted many huge trees that covered the ground with dried, dead foliage so it was impossible for anything over five pounds to mask their movement.

I got up and looked out my window to the right side of the yard and saw nothing. Then, I turned to the left and found myself staring into the face of a hairy monster that, in my frightened, child's mind, was the werewolf from my nightmare.

Midnight screams were a consistent and effective means of summoning my parents and they quickly presented themselves. My father did an annoyed, half-ass check of the outside yard by pulling the curtain back a few inches and scanning the dark for two seconds. It would have been a little more comforting if he had actually looked before he determined that, "There's nothing out there and it was just a dream."

After that night, I never had that nightmare again but I never forgot its connection to the frightening, real experience.

Chapter Six

Could my regressions and projections have simply been dreams? If I've only learned one thing in this lifetime, it's that anything is possible.

Therefore, the practical, rational, left side of my brain switched its focus to dream study and braced itself for Professor Gare's *"Dreams 101-An Introduction to the Subconscious World of Frustrating Symbolism"*.

My early deductions accepted that if spirit truly resides in my subconscious, then dreams were messages from the very soul and well, worth a listen.

I decided to forego the use of instructional cassettes in favor of reading multiple dream definition books, but they proved to be of little assistance. I discovered that not only does the subconscious speak in the language of symbolism, but the *specific* meanings of the symbols are often personally defined by the person receiving the dream. That is, it will often pull from your personal lexicon.

A great example is to ask several different people what kind of symbolism they would attach to a dream about an alligator. Many, perhaps even most, would see a menacing reptile and deem it a symbol of a potential threat.

Personally, I have a deep respect for the alligator. They have stood the test of time and required very little evolvement to survive.

It looks to me like their original blueprint was a solid design.

Symbolically, their exterior is very tough to penetrate, but their interior is as delicate as any other living thing.

Still, determining the symbolic meaning of the content is only half of the chore. The other part requires an answer to the question: what is the action of the symbol?

For example, if the gator were attacking me, I could interpret that as my hard exterior will be off-putting. Or, perhaps I was going to get into some kind of trouble or bad situation in which I needed to remain tough.

If there were several gators swimming around me, I might see that as having many acquaintances, but few or no close friends.

For some, that might signify potential dangers on the horizon.

Perhaps the reptile was simply sunning itself; calm and unmoving as I watched. That could represent a need for some downtime. Perhaps I need some much needed rest or sustenance or to pause and reflect before moving forward. Of course, the specifics of your interpretation's message would reference your personal life circumstances.

Dreaming abundantly and vividly from an early age, I can remember describing my dreams to my parents with exaggerated excitement as if they were real. Mostly, my enthusiasm would be met with a dismissal of any relevance and a conclusive "dreams are not real".

I can't say that I blame my parents since young children often endure terrible nightmares. If young boys and girls believed their dream content to be real, mothers and fathers would rarely sleep. I can accept that dreams are not, secularly, real, but I argue that their messages are quite relevant.

In my current lifetime, I've had more dreams than I could ever recall. Unfortunately, for human sleep requirements, many were nightmares from which I would wake and spend significant time documenting and trying to decode.

A significant series of nightmares that is most engrained in my memory, occurred in June of 2000. I had three disturbing dreams in three consecutive nights, that all had a central theme of death.

The first nightmare displayed a closed casket in an empty funeral home. I tried repeatedly but I could not open it. Desperate to find out which one of my friends had died, I screamed for help but only felt pain and anguish at the loss.

In the second nightmare, I walked through a room filled with dead bodies. There were corpses covering every inch of this large room. Splattered blood covered the walls and the stench of death and decay was sickening. The room was somehow familiar, and I felt that I had been there before, but I did not know any of the dead people.

Rounding out the trio of death dreams was one of…uh, *interesting*, symbolism. I watched myself as I stood over a grave.

I was some sort of sorcerer.

Using my inherent abilities, I levitated a dead man from his coffin. With the ability to wield the spark of life, I surged new life into the decaying corpse. The newly-alive man shook and twitched uncontrollably as he growled and snarled. It was clear that he had been revived with the behavior of an aggressive animal rather than the passive demeanor of a human being. Realizing my failure, I removed the life force with one swift motion of my finger. The empty carcass fell back to the ground.

Again, I raised the corpse of the man into the air and instilled life's breath and heartbeat inside of him. This time, he appeared calm but uncoordinated and lacking the ability to move his arms and legs despite his efforts. I determined that he lacked feeling in his extremities. Another failed attempt warranted the finger motion that restored death. The lifeless body again, fell to the ground.

I repeated the process over and over until I woke up sweating.

For years, I stressed over the meaning of these dreams and was convinced, and unhappy, that they were prophetic.

One of the many, unfortunate side effects of aging is the loss of people in my life. To date, I have mourned the passing of four people; coincidentally, the first three were named, Robert.

The first loss was that of a friend who had moved to Pennsylvania. Despite his relocation, we remained friends and often talked on the phone and kept each other abreast of our life happenings.

I had gotten violently sick after a severe case of food poisoning and was still recovering when his sister called me one Saturday morning. Apparently, Robert had switched his ongoing medications that treated his lifelong illness. He drank one glass of wine at a party the prior evening that had an unfortunate fatal reaction to one of the new drugs. His sister found him dead the next morning.

Due to my weakened condition, I wasn't able to fly to his funeral and the drive from Florida to Pennsylvania was also not an option. I felt guilty for not attending since he had flown from Germany to be at my surprise thirtieth birthday party, just a year prior. I did find some solace, however, in a dream, the day after he passed.

In the dream, I was standing in a solid white room. Robert emerged from the white light wearing a big, happy smile. He looked healthy and vibrant. We hugged and he said "goodbye".

Recalling the first "death dream", I wondered at the symbolism of the closed casket that I was unable to open. Perhaps that represented my lack of attendance at his funeral.

Next, one of the General Managers of the company I worked for committed suicide on Christmas Eve. From what I was told, he shot himself in the head and his remains were to be found all over the walls and floor.

I had only visited his store a few times and didn't know him very well at all. The store was near my home and I decided it would be respectful to attend the service and show my support with the other local employees.

Recalling the second dream of death, I was familiar with the room but not the dead occupants. I'm not trying to place a square peg in a round hole but the symbolism resonates as I was familiar with the store due to my visits, but not the General Manager. Also, the dream depicts bloodied walls and floors that were much like the sickening description of Robert's suicide scene as it was relayed to me.

The third Robert to pass was a neighbor friend of mine who worked as a freelance carpenter and all-around handyman. He was a big, older, Kentucky-born guy with white hair and a big heart.

One summer, I worked with him to earn some side money. At first, I would move the heavy lumber while he crafted wood. After a few weeks he was kind enough to teach me how to build fences and decks. He also explained electrical and plumbing repair. As a result, I learned invaluable skills that saved me thousands on my own home repairs and improvements.

Unfortunately, after successfully beating throat cancer, he passed away from a heart attack. His mother was visiting at the time, and while I was sad at his passing, I was glad that he was with his mom, since they had remained close over the years.

After reading "death dream" number three, I felt the symbolism resonate through me instantly. Robert, or Bob, while open to doing things affordably, was a perfectionist and did quality wood work. If it didn't look right when the job was done, he did it again until it met his standards. Granted, the symbolism of recreating a dead man over and over until they are perfectly human again is dark and morbid, but a craft is a craft.

Unfortunately, I haven't been able to identify all of the recurring symbols in my dreams. To this day, I still dream of white turtles. While a big fan of the reptile, I have never seen a white one, except in my dreams.

Also, I dreamt very clearly of the numbers: 2, 4, 6, 8 and 11. For years I played those five numbers in the state lottery, but I never won. And, last time I checked, those numbers had yet to win. I did, however, research their meanings in the study of numerology and I feel that their individual definitions are not applicable to me.

The fourth person that I've lost in this lifetime is my mother who, not surprisingly, features prominently in some of my most profound experiences, which I'll discuss shortly.

Chapter Seven

I spent much of my retail career staying overnight in hotels. Most were nice while some, not so much.

Achieving the elite, "diamond" status for my ridiculously excessive, annual stays challenged the hotels to leave me with a memorable impression. The lodging eventually became difficult to differentiate and boasted all the same amenities. After many years, it was often only the negative experiences that would remain after a stay.

From a paranormal standpoint, I had a few hotel room experiences, good and bad, that were worth remembering.

My first encounter with a hotel ghost was back in 1996. I was working in Chicago for two straight months for a western apparel and footwear company. I was sent to assess the operations of the store and act as General Manager during my stay. My lodging was at a Best Western.

To this day I remain confused with their name as it certainly wasn't the "best" and there was nothing "western" about it.

The April and May period of my stay delivered seasonally daily rain, so my sightseeing was limited. Consequently, I spent a lot of time in the room reading and would often fall asleep with a book in my hand.

One night, I woke to the sound of movement in my room. With the light still on from reading, I was able to scan the entire room quickly for signs of an intruder, but saw nothing. Then, I heard a soft noise coming from the bathroom.

With my book still in hand, and the delusion that it would be a formidable defensive weapon, I crept toward the bathroom. Luckily, the light switch for the dark bathroom was on the outer wall and I flipped it to the on position. Having left the shower curtain open, I could clearly see that the small washroom was empty. Chalking the noise up to pipes or the occupants of the adjacent room, I turned off the light and turned to go back to bed.

But in the instant that I turned, I found myself face to face, with a Native American. He had long, black hair and a dark, tanned face. His eyebrows were thick and low which helped him deliver a serious, penetrating stare. Only a second later I heard another noise behind me and turned, out of reaction, but quickly realized that the intruder warranted my attention, so I turned back.

He was gone. In the split second it took for me to look back, he had vanished. I searched the room and verified that the door was locked and the windows were secured.

For obvious reasons, I would get very little sleep for the remainder of the night.

The next day I was walking the sales floor of the store when a woman entered through the front glass door. I watched her walk past two associates and straight to me. In a very surreal moment, the woman looked at me, smiled and said, "I'm half Indian."

She then turned and left the store.

By this point, I would have expected Dane to block my sometimes frantic, daily calls but, later that night while I sat in my hotel room, he answered.

Psychically, he connected with his guide, and perhaps, even with the spirit in my room. His assertion was that the Native American's intentions were that of protection. Furthermore, I would be well advised to honor him, with a gift.

I wasn't really sure how I would do that, exactly, but I accepted the advice, nonetheless. Understandably, I was more willing to accept the presence of a ghost as a protector in lieu of one with ill intentions. Luckily, there were no visitors in my room that night and I was able to catch up on my sleep.

The next day, I was working behind the counter when a man walked in. He seemed lost and I asked him if he required my assistance. He looked at me, smiled and then proceeded to browse through the gift table that housed candles, shoe horns and various décor made with steer horns.

He picked up a black candleholder that backlit the silhouette of a Native American on a horse. Walking it over to me, he smiled again and asked, "How much is this?"

I took the candle from him and scanned the barcode. After telling him the price, his smile widened broadly and then he exited the store, leaving me standing there and holding the candle.

I deduced that I had been shown the gift that I would deliver to my hotel room protector. I purchased the candle and burned it every night before I went to sleep in hope of being protected.

While I never saw the Native American again, I did have several dreams of him while in Chicago.

The dreams were mostly the same. I would see him standing either in front of me or beside me. The Native American was stoic with lowered eyebrows and unblinking eyes. He stared at me with his arms crossed and never spoke to me. Once I arrived back to Florida, the dreams ended.

The most intense hotel room experience occurred in 2013. While staying overnight in what I call an "off-brand hotel chain," I shared a room with a co-worker who, out of respect for his privacy, I will refer to as, Joe.

Normally, I would have stayed at a Hilton Garden Inn, but we were attending a meeting downstairs in the privately- owned hotel's presentation room. Out of convenience, and their very, inexpensive rate, we booked a room with them.

At around 4 o'clock in the morning, I was abruptly ripped from my sleep by the loud, agitated moaning and mumbling of my roommate. I called out to Joe several times until he finally woke up. Joe sat up in his bed and composed himself before he described the chilling particulars of his nightmare.

He told me that he had found himself standing beside his bed and could see his sleeping, physical body. The room was glowing with a reddish hue. Looking over at me, he found that the hotel room dresser had me pinned down on my bed.

According to Joe, the brown, wooden dresser was lying across my body as if it had been placed there to restrict my movement. He explained that I looked at him, then down at the large piece of furniture across my chest and then back at him in disbelief.

The last expression I wore was one of desperation as we both realized that there was something growling in the shadows behind him. The snarls and heavy, rough breathing instilled within us the fear of an evil creature with harmful intent. Unable to see the beast, Joe swung his fists, blindly and angrily at the darkness. It was here that I woke him up.

We briefly discussed the obvious presence of a negative energy in the room. Our chests were tight and we both felt as if we were being watched. The energy in the room was heavy and the air was much colder than it had been previously.

Joe's impression was that he had astral projected himself out of his body after sensing an intruding energy. At the realization that I would not be able to assist him, he went on the offensive. It was more than unsettling for me to hear that my astral body had been restrained by an astral desk and I was unable to defend myself.

There's something you don't say every day.

After a few more minutes of discussion, we both calmed down; at least enough to fall back to sleep.

Twenty minutes later, he would return the favor and wake me from experiencing a very, realistic nightmare, indicated by my loud moans and garbled yelling.

In my dream, I found myself in the kitchen of the house in which I lived during my junior and high school years. There were glass doors that led out to a screened lanai and adjacent to those was a door that led to the garage.

In the nightmare, I watched as four men sat on the covered patio in metal folding chairs, laughing at me. But it wasn't just laughter. They wore expressions of disdain and laughed in contempt of my very existence. They looked upon me as worthless and despicable for reasons I didn't know.

I found this incredibly hurtful and tried to scream for them to stop, but I was mute. I strained to speak but my voice was gone. Unable to express myself, I stood and endured their ridicule and hatred in their malevolent gestures.

My pained face told them that I was confused and terrified at finding that I could not speak. At this, they pointed and laughed even harder.

I turned to see the handle on the door to the garage being turned and assumed that it was another intruder. The door opened outward into the garage, so I grabbed the handle and pulled it shut. Again, the doorknob turned and the door opened slightly. With frustration, I grabbed the handle and met forceful resistance as I tried to close the door. I continued to struggle against an unseen force until it finally allowed me to pull the door closed and lock it.

    I was terrified at what was trying to enter my home. I felt violated and in an odd, terrifying sense, hunted.

    Suddenly, the top left corner of the door fell to the floor. I watched as more and more of the door was being ripped away by an invisible force that was hell bent on getting to me. Presuming that it was an invisible demon and finally finding my voice, I screamed for help. It was here that my roommate woke me up.

After relaying my disturbing nightmare to Joe, we talked for another thirty minutes about the negativity that was wreaking havoc in our room.

Our room seemed darker. Movement out of the corners of our eyes kept us awake and guessing as to the evil being's next move.

We knew something was taunting us but with only another hour or so before we would need to get up and prepare for the day, we endured the fear in lieu of changing rooms.

The same night, I would have one more nightmare after I finally fell back into a short slumber, but I would wake from it silently.

In the last nightmare, Joe was in the bathroom getting ready for the day. While I was getting dressed in the room, something caught my eye on the floor by the hotel room door. I looked down to see a skeleton hand crawling toward me.

Given the overuse of severed hands in movies and television shows, I was hesitant to believe my eyes, but it was very realistic with portions of skin still attached, so I couldn't help but believe it to be real. Additionally, it was heading toward me quickly and the fingers walked the hand with the movement of a tarantula.

Later, Joe and I determined that there was indeed, someone or something in the room that did not want us there.

Don't worry, evil-thing, I won't be back.

Chapter Eight

Hotels are dirty in more than just one way, but mostly, they contain varying amounts of negative energy.

Ouija Boards are portals that allow negative entities passage into our world.

Assuming the two previous statements are true, most intelligent pupils would deduce that it is unwise to use the Ouija Board in a hotel room.

I've always been an average student.

In my defense, I was operating out of the misinformed misunderstanding that as long as you tell the board that nothing but good is allowed to come through, then all negative spirits' entry will be blocked.

Joe and I were, again, staying overnight on business and he reluctantly agreed to use the board. His agreement was based solely on my assurance that only "spirits of the light" will be contacted.

To our surprise, a very nasty and threatening entity came through the board. The pointer spelled out words such as *die*, and *burn in hell*. Suffice to say, he was less than happy with me which prompted him to tell me of his childhood encounter.

When Joe was fourteen, he and three of his neighborhood friends were hanging out in his best friend's basement. It was well after dark on a typical, snowy, Michigan, winter night. Out of boredom, his best bud, Mike, brought out a Ouija Board and suggested that they all play.

It didn't take long before the plastic pointer responded to the gang's innocent questions. They laughed in amazement as the pointer moved itself across the slick board.

First, the board replied with accurate birthdates of the teen kids.

Second, middle names were spelled out across the board. The young adults gasped in exhilarated excitement at the eerie, accurate responses.

The initial, innocent responses quickly became a threatening and morbid prediction.

The board, unprompted by a question, moved its pointer from letters to numbers until a date was revealed: May 7th, 2001.

Assuming the message was meant for him as they were in his home, Mike asked the board to explain the significance of the date to which he received the following reply:

"That is the day that I will take your soul."

Mikes shrieked as he and his friends withdrew their fingers from the plastic pointer. At that same moment, a black cat appeared in the basement window and screeched at them. A cold wind rushed through the basement and extinguished the single candle that had been providing the only source of illumination. Mike's younger sister screamed as her long, blond hair stood straight up, above her head.

Mike scurried to corner of the room and turned on a lamp. The cat was gone, the cold air had dissipated and his sister's hair once again, lay flat on her head.

After hearing of Joe's terrifying night, I asked the obvious question regarding the prophetic death date of May 7th, 2011. Sadly, Mike had died of cancer on that day.

What I have learned from my personal use of the board is that is uses the information in my mind to answer our questions. Joe and I tested the board repeatedly and it always spelled out what I was thinking. However, it could not read *his* mind.

I still don't know why the board only had access to my thoughts. Perhaps I am more open to spirit and therefor they can enter into my energy field. Given Joe's past experience I can completely understand that he would be closed off to the invading energies.

I also considered that spirits coming through the board are actually joining their energies with mine and Joe acted as a kind of ground for the union. That may also help to explain why the board often works most effectively with two or more people.

Regardless, it only seemed to have access to the knowledge inside my head and I didn't see any reason to continue using the board.

After several months had passed I stumbled across the "game" box that housed the Ouija board as I was searching through paperwork in my nightstand. Feeling that I needed to dispose of it once and for all, I took the box to the dining room table.

I had developed a habit of staging items on my rarely used table for future errands such as outgoing mail, dry cleaning, etc.

An hour or so later Joe arrived to my house for a visit before we would leave for the gym. Once inside, he immediately spotted the box which contained the board on the table and asked, rhetorically, "Really?"

I smiled and explained, "Relax, I'm giving it away." For no conscious reason, I removed the lid from the box. At the very instant that the board was revealed, my three dogs, in unison, rushed toward the table.

A large, fully-coated Chow Chow mix, a handsome square-headed black Lab and a medium sized Pit Bull mix, that, to this day, desperately wants to be the alpha, chased after *something* down the hallway. They all were seemingly in pursuit of an entity that was unseen to our human eyes. The pack was abruptly stopped by the closed door of the front bedroom. For the next five minutes my dogs barked and sniffed at the small opening at the bottom of the door. I watched and listened to them whine and growl in desperation to get to what was behind it.

Joe and I remained silent as we each processed what had transpired in front of us. I asked him to relay his account of what had happened.

"You took the lid off of the box and something must have jumped out because the dogs ran after it. It looked like they chased something invisible down the hallway and then it disappeared into the front bedroom."

That's exactly what I thought happened.

My dogs had clearly caught a scent or, and perhaps more accurately, a *sense* of something that had escaped the confines of the box. Assuming that was the case, it had cowered into the room, temporarily safe behind the closed door.

From my experience, I believe that the board is a portal for travel from the astral plane to the physical plane. Furthermore, it's an all-access entry for light beings, dark entities, human spirits and classic demons. In other words, anyone and anything can pass through.

The idea that the portal could be, somehow, left open and allow random beings to wander through seemed plausible. I used this terrifying concept for the story basis in *7 Apparitions*.

Chapter Nine

It was the summer of 1999 and after years of renting, I was looking to buy a house.

The realtor received my requirements of a home with three bedrooms, two bathrooms, a pool and a selling price of less than one hundred thousand dollars.

She ran a search through her listings and suggested a subdivision that I had actually lived in for a year after my parent's divorce. Hardly fond of the area, I declined even considering a house in that neighborhood. However, after a few unsuccessful months of house hunting, she circled back to my black-listed subdivision and I gave in.

It was the beginning of September when I looked at a house that met all of my criteria and even boasted a lake view.

The house was owned by a woman who had moved to Maryland. During a recent separation and pending divorce from her husband, he had died and she was selling it, "as is". While the structure of the home appeared solid, the walls were in need of paint, the carpets were soiled and the pool water was a dark green. The unclear water concerned me as it hid any potential damage to the pool itself and may have been in need of costly repair.

I soon discovered that the house had been sitting empty and clearly ignored for several months, which was the apparent cause of its desperate need of cleaning.

One thing, in particular, that disturbed me was that the front bedroom carpet was so badly stained that it was almost completely black. I recall wondering if someone had spilled motor oil.

I had planned on replacing the carpet anyway, so I made an offer for exactly the price that she was asking. As long as the house passed the structural inspection and the pool didn't leak, it would still be a great deal.

Within a few days, the owner countered with a significantly increased price and cited that there had been "heavy interest in the house." Apparently she felt she could get more than her original asking price.

No thanks.

Over the next three weeks, the continued house-hunt yielded nothing of interest. Then, the seller's realtor called and asked if I was still interested. I decided to see the house again.

To my delight, the walls had been freshly painted, the carpets had been replaced and the pool was crystal clear. I submitted an offer that was much lower than the inflated price with which she had countered. To my delight, my offer was even slightly lower than my original bid and it was accepted.

The closing on the house occurred late in October and I moved in during the Halloween weekend, despite my initial blockade.

"Buyers are liars." The realtor joked and then stated that her intention was *not* to be crass.

It sounded crass.

A few days prior to the move, I enlisted the support of my friend, Carl to assist with some minor work. We needed to install new window blinds, closet shelves, ceiling fans and bathroom mirrors.

For some reason, the bathroom mirrors were missing.

Needing additional supplies, I left him at the house and drove to the local Home Depot. When I returned, I found him lying flat on the carpet in the living room and engaged in conversation. He was more than startled when he saw me walk through the front door.

Carl suffered from a bad back. According to him, he was hurting from being on the ladder all morning, so he had laid down on the carpet to stretch out his back.

He then claims he heard me and assumed that I had returned from the hardware store. He began a dialogue with a voice that responded to him from the front bedroom.

"Gare, I'm taking a break. My back is killing me."

A voice asked. "What are you working on?"

Carl replied, "Hanging new blinds over the sliding glass doors."

"What was wrong with the old ones?" asked the voice.

Carl laughed. "I don't know. I guess you like to spend money."

Just then I appeared through the front door. Carl turned his head and could not reconcile that I had just then returned.

"Where were you?" Carl asked, startled and confused.

I carried in bags of screws and other needed items. "I told you, Home Depot."

Carl slowly and painfully sat up and looked down the hallway at the front bedroom. "Then, who have I been talking to?"

Carl relayed his short conversation with the voice and the hairs on the back of my neck stood up. More than curious, he got up and we both walked, slowly, to the front bedroom, only to find it empty.

Confused and finding no explanation, we returned to work. Then, Carl realized that his hammer was no longer on his tool belt. With the exception of our tools, the shelves and ceiling fans, the house was empty. We had not moved in any boxes, furniture, household items, etc. He had been using his hammer in the same room in which we stood just minutes prior to me coming back from the hardware store. We searched the entire, empty house. It had vanished and, to this day, we have not found it.

During lunch, we ate in the backyard to enjoy the view of the small lake. The landscaping was sparse, but the yard boasted eight giant, lush queen palms. As I surveyed the lot, I imagined the tropical green, yellow and red foliage I would plant. Soon, a colorful landscape would replace the unsightly, grey dirt.

My eyes caught a glimpse of something white on the ground. I walked over to see a display both haunting and disturbing and immediately called Dane.

I described my find to Dane on my cell phone as I stood over an unsettling sight.

"There are dozens of white and grey bird feathers placed flat on the ground. They're arranged like a fan, but a full 360 degrees." Being an animal lover, I felt a tinge of sadness as I continued the description. "In the center, oh my God, it's a beak of a small bird."

Dane remained unemotional despite my growing discomfort. "What else?"

I continued. "The sharp ends of the feathers are all pointing to the tiny mouth. In each corner around the feathers are four small, white rocks." I became agitated along with a sense of trepidation as the parts of a dead bird stared back at me. "What the hell is this?"

Dane's voice was now heavy with concern. "How long has it been there?"

"I don't know. I just noticed it today." I replied, frustrated and trying to determine a timeframe.

We had walked the entire lot the day of closing and had stood just a few feet from where the feathers were. Surely, we would have seen it then if it had been there. In all honesty, I couldn't be sure.

I asked him repeatedly to explain what he thought it was, but he refused. Instead, he urged me to obtain sea salt and cover the area with it.

While I assumed that this was some kind of ritualistic display, I had never seen one before, let alone on my property. There was a strange and terrifying sense of a personal attack or warning surrounding the find. Which is odd since the house sat vacant for over four months and the one surviving owner didn't even care enough to return and oversee the sale. Who would have any interest in the house now and what would they have against me?

I returned the next day with sea salt and soon the display of bird feathers turned into a white mound of a cleansing condiment.

Despite my research, I could not find any reference to a ritualistic display similar to what I had found.

I moved in the following Saturday, which happened to be the day before Halloween. Capitalizing on the opportunity to deter any future vandalism, I bought only brand name candy bars to win over the neighborhood kids.

I was basically bribing them to *not* egg my house.

My buddy, Dirk, was helping me unload the truck when a group of children rode their bicycles up the driveway and stopped just outside the garage.

Apparently, the unloading of boxes and furniture out of a moving truck didn't paint a clear enough picture as one of the young boys asked, "Are you moving in?"

I don't dislike conversations with children. But, I prefer to have them with bright children.

"Uh, yeah." I delivered, somewhat facetiously, while I motioned my eyes to the moving truck. Then, just to be a dick, I rolled my eyes at Dirk and turned to walk away from the kids.

"Do you know the history of the house?" the boy asked. His follow-up question would not receive my rolling eyes of dismissal, this time. In fact, his far-too-eager tone suggested he had at least a little bit on intel that might be of interest to me.

Cautiously, I replied, "No."

Without hesitation and with way too much enthusiasm, he blurted, "It's haunted!"

Dirk burst into laughter. "You bought the Amityville House!"

Great, now I had to address two children.

I leered at Dirk. "Really?"

I walked up to the young boy, who was visibly trembling while trying to contain his excitement. Fearing he might pee in his pants, I quickly asked, "Ok, what happened here?"

The little kid took center stage as he leaned back on his bike and folded his arms in front of him. The other children stared at him expectantly. I imagined that they had all heard his story at least once before but their eyes were wide with anticipation as he told us of his first-hand experience.

"The man that lived here killed himself and I found him!"

A suicide in the home that I had just purchased was definitely not what I was expecting him to say. I assumed that he had seen a ghost in the window or maybe the lights flickered on and off late at night inside a known-empty house. Certainly, I never imagined that he would proclaim that he had found a dead body.

Out of the corner of my eye, I saw Dirk take a few steps closer so he could hear the child better.

The boy looked to the wall of the garage to his left. "He shot himself in the front bedroom. There's the bullet hole."

I tilted my head and narrowed my eyes as belief began to root itself inside my mind. After walking over to the garage wall I noted that the hole was located on the drywall, just above my waistline. The opposite, interior wall was, indeed, in the front bedroom.

As if a class bell had rung, the group of children abruptly left. Without uttering a word, Dirk and I went inside the house and headed straight for the bedroom.

I ran my finger along the drywall near the height of my waistline. It wasn't long before I found a cold, round pocket of undried putty. I pushed my finger into it with ease. My friend remained quiet and left the room in favor of resuming the unpacking of the truck. As I followed behind him, I recalled the severely stained carpet that had been replaced by the time of my second visit. It was clear that those permeating, dark stains had been blood.

The young, neighborhood informant returned to my house the next night in costume and in search of Halloween candy. He was accompanied by his mother, who introduced herself as my next door neighbor.

A few days later, I arrived home as she was working in her yard. I seized the opportunity to get the backstory on the incident. At first, the subject matter was uncomfortable for her and she was reluctant to discuss it. But, in the end, she felt that I, as the new owner, deserved to know.

Or, I was overbearing and she felt that if she told me what I wanted to know, I would cease my relentless questioning.

Yeah, that sounds more likely.

She told me that a childless couple had owned the house prior to my purchase.

In respect of their privacy, I'll refer to them as Rick and Carol in lieu of using their real names.

The story goes that Carol, who the neighbors had generally considered to be crazy, left Rick and filed for divorce.

Carol was known to be emotionally unstable and even abusive at times. Neighbors described her taking morning walks up and down the street in her bath robe while chastising anyone in her path for their glares of judgment. I also heard that she had a soft spot for stray cats. This was easily confirmed when I woke to countless feral felines huddled in my backyard awaiting food. It took only a short introduction to my dogs for the kitties to relocate.

Rick became depressed and his behavior suggested that he was also losing a little of his own sanity.

Shortly after Carol's departure, Rick began approaching the neighbors and offering them his furniture and personal belongings. He told them that he would rather they have it than allow the lawyers to take it all from him. One neighbor claims that Rick told him that he had flushed ten thousand dollars down the toilet in an effort to keep his wealth from the attorneys.

I heard this story more than once. In one version, the money had been given away and in another, he hid it in the walls of the house.

Despite my inclination to put a hammer to the drywall, I never looked.

Rick held a part time job at a department store and worked every Tuesday and Thursday. He claimed it was "something to do".

The remainder of his time was spent lamenting, to anyone who would listen, about his impending divorce and how he cared for his dog; a giant breed mix of a Great Pyrenees and a Golden Retriever.

Rick was also known to help the neighborhood children with their bicycle repairs. For all intents and purposes he was considered to be a nice, albeit distraught, guy.

Rick was unusually home one Thursday morning and retrieving something from the trunk of his car when one of the neighbors saw him. When asked why he wasn't at work, he explained that he had a dentist appointment. According to the neighbor, that was the last time Rick was seen alive.

Two days later, the young boy from next door required assistance with his bike. Rick's car was in the driveway so he proceeded to his front door. Surprised to find an open door, the child rang the doorbell and called out to Rick, but he only heard the barks of Rick's dog from the backyard. When Rick didn't appear after the boy's follow-up knock, he decided to enter the house.

He stood at the end of the long hallway that led to the front bedroom with his mouth agape as he witnessed a gruesome scene.

Rick's lifeless body was sprawled across the blood stained carpet. The walls were washed red while bits and pieces of his head peppered a ten food radius. A gun rested in his lap; the obvious cause of the tragic death.

Terrified, the boy ran to get his mother. She returned to behold the same horrific atrocity and immediately called the authorities.

Later, my neighbor would recall the small table, to the right of Rick's body and in front of the small closet. It held several burning candles and multiple pictures of his estranged wife. She described it as a shrine that was adorned with many strange objects including chicken's feet, tiny, homemade dolls, and small bags tied with twine. In the center of the display was a handwritten note that read, "Carol, you win."

Suddenly, the dead bird offering in my backyard appeared to have some relevance.

I called Dane and explained the home's recent sad and disturbing history. He walked me through the process of "cleaning" a house. That is, a spiritual and energy cleansing, using salt, sage, white candles and lemons.

After lighting the end of a sage smudge wand I moved through my house. Committed to reach every corner, nook and cranny with the heavy scent of sage, I opened closet doors, shower curtains and even cabinets. Next, I moved through my home holding a white candle. While rotating it in front of me, I envisioned the residual negativity being sucked into the candle and shot up and out to the ethers where it would dissipate. The glass surrounding the candle warmed in my hand and soon the temperature in the house increased five to six degrees.

 I applied salt to every window sill and doorway, both inside and outside my home. As I followed Dane's instructions I recalled a particular channeling session in which his guide explained the necessity of continuous cleansing.

"Think of negativity as insects and bugs that find their way into homes in search of food and living space."

Dane's head swiveled back and forth in an even movement. His eyes remained closed but the lids fluttered as if trying to pry themselves open. The woman's voice boomed from his mouth as she enunciated every other syllable.

"You use chemicals to chase away the unwanted pests and cleaning formulas to create an inhospitable environment. This is not dissimilar to the cleansing of a home of undesirable entities using sage, salt and holy water."

She paused and a pleased smile appeared on Dane's face. "Those pesky creatures return when the chemicals have dissipated, surely enticed by the dirty dishes left in the kitchen sink."

The smile on Dane's face was replaced with raised eyebrows as she continued. "To complete our analogy, the dark beings are lured to your living space by your negative moods and behavior. Indeed, contrary to popular belief, like attracts like."

Having recalled the session on cleansing, it made much more sense now that I was actually applying the practices with the sage, candle and salt.

Getting back to the task at hand, I placed half slices of lemons in each corner of the front bedroom for a period of seven days. A successful cleansing would produce black lemons as they would have absorbed all the negative energy. A week later, I found that the lemon's color remained unchanged.

Uh-oh.

After talking with Dane, he suggested I try again. I decided I would repeat the cleaning process the very next morning.

I was unaware that later that night, I would receive a message that whatever was in the house, was definitely still there.

After dinner that evening, I moved to my office and sat at my desk working, or rather, playing on my computer. To my right was a closed window that provided a view of the courtyard. Normally, at night, I kept the blinds closed for privacy and this evening was no exception. As usual, my faithful black Lab, Sobek, slept below the window, just a few feet away from me.

I was surfing the internet and felt like I was being watched. I grew more and more uncomfortable and was certain someone was standing next to me. I tried to shake off the fear when the window blinds made a startling noise. Stunned, I jumped out of my chair. It was as if someone had taken their hand and smacked them from right to left. After hearing the sound of the hit, I watched as the blinds swung back and forth and produced the scraping sound of their interaction. It occurred to me that my office is adjacent to the front bedroom. In fact, the closet in my office aligns with the closet in the bedroom.

Was there a correlation?

Similar to the night from my childhood when my bed levitated itself, Sobek also reacted, which helped solidify my belief in the uncanny occurrence. If the dog also saw and/or heard it, it couldn't have been my imagination.

My agitated dog, jolted out of slumber, emitted a low growl and was on all fours while sniffing the air for an explanation. Eventually, the blinds slowed their movement and rested back into place.

To appease the rational left side of my brain, I reviewed the environmental particulars. Aside from the pups, I was home alone. The ceiling fan was off and the air conditioning had not yet kicked on to cool the house for the night. I was awake and alert and had not been drinking or taken any mind-altering substances.

It boils down to this. The blinds were moving after I heard them being hit. Something or someone did it because window treatments don't move by themselves. It wasn't me and it wasn't my sleepy retriever. I am reminded of a borrowed quote I heard in a Star Trek movie:

"If you eliminate the impossible, whatever remains, however improbable, must be the truth."

Many would find it improbable that I agitated an unfriendly spirit when I performed a failed, cleansing process, but, not impossible.

Early the next morning, I attempted to clean the front bedroom and entire house once again. While I waited for the darkening of the lemon halves over the next week, I experienced some more unsettling activity.

For days, things went missing and were never to be found. Included in the list is a check, a set of keys, my driver's license, and even a new license plate for my truck.

I distinctly recall placing the plate on my desk. Later that day, I found the appropriate screwdriver but when I returned to retrieve the plate, it was no longer there. It was metal and measured around four by ten inches, yet it had vanished.

At the end of the seven day period, I found that the lemons were still quite yellow. I became frustrated and paced the bedroom. It was cold, indeed, much colder than the rest of the house.

I've read that entities can basically suck the energy out of a room and even people. They may use the stolen energy to manipulate physical reality, such as taking keys and license plates, and even manifest themselves. The thought caused me to recall Dane's and his guide's agreement of her use of his physical body.

Dane would be overwhelmed with a positive energy after channeling his guide. It was easy for me to conclude that my moods and behavior could be easily affected by the particular entities that surround me. That gave me even more fervor to remove the negativity in my home.

I closed the air conditioning vent which redirected the cooled air to other parts of the house. My goal was to test my theory that if the room remained cold without air conditioning, something else was dropping the temperature.

The bedroom maintained a cold and heavy atmosphere for days afterward and I had my answer.

After another call to Dane, he agreed to come over the next day and tackle the negativity, himself.

I thanked him profusely, hung up and called the realtor who had listed the house. It seemed to me that there would be a clause, or even a law that required sellers to disclose the occurrences of a suicide or murder in a home on the market. I was half right. Full disclosure is required in some states, but not in good, old Florida.

Hiding behind the law, the realtor copped a slight attitude and asked me if it would have changed my decision to buy the home if I had known about the unfortunate event.

Without hesitation, I replied, "Probably not, but I would have offered less for it. And, morally, don't you think you should have told me?"

Not surprisingly, my direct question abruptly ended the conversation.

When Dane arrived to my house the next morning, I was surprised to see that he was beyond pissed off.

He told me that whoever or whatever was in the front bedroom, had gone to his apartment the night before and attacked him. Dane explained that he was relaxing on his couch and watching television when the room temperature dropped to, what felt like, freezing. He could see his breath in the frigid air when, suddenly, he felt pain run from the bottom of his feet to the top of his head. He writhed in agony for several seconds and heard a deep, sinister voice in his ear, telling him to "stay away." Then, the pain disappeared and the temperature in the room returned to normal.

What concerned Dane the most was that the entity had the ability to enter his apartment. He explained that he routinely performs rituals and protects his living space from any unwanted spirits, good or bad. This dark entity was disturbingly strong enough to break through his protective barriers and well aware of our intentions to banish it.

Dane had come prepared with a printed ritual that required our mutual participation. After hours of salting, smudging, chanting, and candle burning, we felt that we had succeeded in banishing the negative spirit.

The following morning at three o'clock, I woke up to see something that would prove that our banishing efforts had failed. I was unprepared for the unholy encounter that would haunt me for the rest of my life.

I opened my eyes to see a grossly burned demon staring coldly at me. Its face was hot red with burned folds of skin running from its forehead down to its neck. Piercing yellow eyes targeted a palpable hate at me. The demonic being was only inches from my face and reeked of sulfur.

The demon leaned over my bed with its claw-like hands on both sides of my body. I suddenly realized that I was paralyzed and unable to feel my limbs. Frightening panic engulfed my sense of being. Unable to access my voice, I strained, unsuccessfully, to speak. Inside my head, I cried out for help.

Unbelievably, the demon's expression reacted to my inner cries and pulled back. In the same instant, I sat up, screaming at the top of lungs for help. Sobek, who was at the foot of my bed, was jolted awake at my outburst. He looked up at me, confused.

Suddenly, our attention was pulled to the front of the house where we heard a "thud" from the front bedroom.

Understandably, it took a few minutes for me to gather the courage to investigate the sound.

Finally, I adopted a defensive posture at the intrusion into my bedroom. I grabbed a bat and jumped out of bed.

With a hardly effective weapon against a ghost in my hand, I walked toward the front bedroom only to be stopped at the beginning of the hallway. The obvious reason for the loud sound stared back at me as I found the door to the front bedroom closed.

My fear quickly became anger and I flung open the bedroom door. With a baseball bat on my shoulder and a "get the hell out of my house" expression, I peered into darkness. The room was empty. Despite the closed air conditioning vent, I felt its cold air seep out at me.

The next day, Dane was kind enough to attempt, one more time, a spirit removal. He arrived to my house armed with a ritual that included prayers and some kind of binding spell. I sat this one out, but he was successful in securing the entity to a small corner of the closet, with no access to the bedroom or the remainder of the house. His hope was that with restricted movement, it would leave to find a more hospitable environment.

It was better than nothing.

Over the years, there has been some minor activity such as missing objects and noises but nothing egregious. I did take notice that it was during house renovations that the harmless ghost parlor tricks of lost keys and knocks on the walls, would occur.

After a visit from an impartial, unknown psychic, my assumptions were confirmed. Yes, we bound the demon and it did not have access to the living space in the house, but, I still had at least, one ghost. It was a lost soul.

The psychic woman identified the ghost as Rick, the previous owner, who had committed suicide in the front bedroom.

She went on to explain that Rick had been using some sort of voodoo magic in an attempt to bring back his wife. Unfortunately, he inadvertently conjured a demon, which remained after his passing.

The clairvoyant tried to connect with Rick and show him the way to his light and help him cross over.

I truly hope Rick found peace.

Chapter Ten

As an adult, I was always close to my mom. I helped her with the shopping, the errands, the doctor visits and essentially anything that she needed. We were very much alike as we shared the same sense of humor and direct, no-nonsense demeanor.

Her passing in August of 2009 was, to say the least, devastating. It has me taken this long to build the emotional strength to discuss the spiritual circumstances surrounding her life and death. The time now seems necessary as it's only in hindsight that I am able to understand the significance of the events.

In February, seven months prior to my mother's passing, I had a very vivid, albeit short and simple dream. I was standing in an empty, white room. There was no furniture, nothing hanging on the walls and no doors or windows. I stared at the empty space for what seemed like minutes when a voice suddenly and very loudly spoke to me and said, "Greensboro." Then, I woke up.

My curiosity quite stimulated, I racked my brain to determine the significance of the name. An obvious direction to go was the city in North Carolina. My job at the time took me there four times a year, but nothing unusual or fantastic had happened during my prior trips or the visit after the dream.

A few months later in May, I dreamt that I was standing in a beautiful, spacious field. The trees were all shades of reds and orange while gusty winds sounded their way through their leaves. The ground was a sea of fluorescent green, summer rye. I watched as several loose dogs played with each other just twenty yards to my left. On my right, I caught the image of a young woman walking quite a distance away from me. As I watched her, she turned her head slightly, just before disappearing into the colorful foliage.

Unable to discern her image from so far away, I ran to catch up with her and found her walking down a trail through the majestic, towering trees. My momentum was halted, however, when I was stopped short at the appearance of a blinding white light. She turned and looked at me again and I could clearly see her face. It was Julia.

I woke up and quickly documented the specifics of the dream before they left my short-term memory. While I understood Julia to be a love from a past life and the white light boasted obvious symbolism, I didn't understand the inherent message.

Sometime in June, about a month later, I had gone to my mother's house for a visit. She had a wide-eyed look of amazement on her face when I arrived. Before I could inquire as to the reason for her look of astonishment, she immediately told me about her early morning experience.

My mother characteristically woke up around five o'clock in the morning. While walking out of her bedroom she stopped and opened the blinds over the large living room window. She stood and stared at what she described as one of the most amazing things that she had ever seen.

A beautiful angel sat on top of an overly large, bright moon in the early morning sky. The long blond-haired angel smiled lovingly at my mother for several minutes. Positive that she was dreaming, my mom blinked and rubbed her eyes but the angel and the brilliant moon remained.

A few seconds later, my mother's cat ran past her along the tile and stole her attention. She looked down and then back out the window, but the angel was gone. All that remained was the bright illumination of the moon.

My mom had never talked about ghosts or angels or anything paranormal or spiritual with me. She was very grounded and secular in her perspectives. I felt the emotion in her voice as she described her experience and it was obvious that it had affected her. There was, understandably, a little confusion and shock at what she had seen. She smiled as she told me how moved she was by the warm feeling of love she felt from the angel who smiled down upon her so beautifully.

I knew, in that moment, the reason for the angelic visit; my mother would be passing on. I don't know why I interpreted the angel's visit as a prophetic message, but I knew it with all my being, to be truth.

I held back my thoughts and building emotions in favor of denial. All I could do was remain quiet as she enjoyed the residual feelings of love in the telling of her spiritual experience.

For the duration of my visit, our subsequent conversations would, for the first time, be metaphysical in nature. She had never seen a ghost before but didn't necessarily deny that they existed.

I asked her if she had ever had a recurring dream.

She told me that, for years, she would dream that she was a young girl on a wagon. Native Americans had attacked the wagon train and murdered every single man and woman. In the dream, she could see her dead parents, bloodied and still on the ground. She was crying as she looked up to see a Native American on a horse with his arrow pointed directly at her. Luckily, she would wake up before the arrow was released.

It took everything I had to keep my mouth shut. I never did tell her that I too had a recurring dream.

I was a Native American who sat on top of a horse, staring into the tearful eyes of a young girl as I a pulled back my arrow.

Some would cite coincidence where our dreams were concerned. To them, I would suggest a crowbar to pry open their minds.

I had regressed into several past lives and uncovered some of the reasons for my current behaviors and particular attitudes in this lifetime. It was not a far leap to connect to another in the dream state in which a previous dynamic with my mother was revealed.

Certainly, had I killed her as the dream or, rather, memory suggests, it would explain my behavior as caretaker. I would have carried with me, into this lifetime, feelings of guilt and remorse along with the karmic need for balance. Indeed, for having taken her life, I would provide and care for her until her last day. This is exactly what I did.

A few weeks later, I flew to North Carolina for a week since my job required quarterly audits of every store in my territory. When I arrived to the Greensboro location, I braced myself for what I was certain would be a life altering spiritual experience. Disappointingly, the store visit was business as usual.

I left the store and began my trek to the next city that was almost an hour away. I drove the rental car on cruise control and enjoyed the beautiful scenery that the state boasts.

It wasn't long before I almost lost control of my rental car at the shock of what I saw next. To my right was the same open field that I saw in my dream. The images of the colorful trees, the summer rye grass and even a parting in the foliage, which was the beginning of a trail, came flooding back to my mind as I unbelievably beheld every one of them in my waking state.

I pulled over and gawked in disbelief. If I wasn't completely speechless, the running dogs that appeared, like those in my dream, out of nowhere, stifled any audible comments.

After a few more minutes of head shaking, I got back in the car and drove to the final store of the day. Later, at the hotel, I documented the experience, unknowing that I would soon understand the significance of Greensboro.

On a Sunday night in mid-July, I went to bed a little after eleven o'clock. Sometime during my slumber, I had a disturbing dream about my mother.

I dreamed that she was in my living room and I was on the other side of the house. She was trying to get my attention but I was busy with other people. I finally got free and walked over to her. She took me outside and pointed to the top of the front bedroom. With a terrified expression, she told me, "He is trying to get me." Suddenly, her image shook and became distorted, almost like a hologram that was losing its projection.

My blackberry phone automatically turned off at eleven o'clock p.m. and turned back on at seven o'clock a.m. I wouldn't know if I had received a phone call during that time period until the next morning. I woke up at seven-thirty and found that I had a voice mail.

The message was from my mother. She woke up in the middle of the night with severe chest pains and informed me that she planned on calling 911. I called her cell and home line, but there was no answer.

Immediately, and in a panic, I drove to her house expecting the worst. She wasn't home. I quickly found out that she had called 911 and was stabilized in a nearby hospital, after having suffered a heart attack.

In the coming week, she would undergo heart surgery, spend two weeks in the hospital in recovery and then be released and stay with me.

A week into her continued recovery at my home, she began to have mini seizures. She would lose the time and not remember anything while she was seizing. Afterward, she would be disoriented and understandably agitated.

On the evening of August 9th, 2009, I helped my mother into bed and she immediately had a short, mini seizure. However, this time, when she came out of it, she was smiling and appeared tranquil and calm. My mother looked at me with a loving smile and spoke evenly in a soothing tone and told me, "It's alright, now. You're a good son and I love you."

Her words, while loving and kind, set off an alarm in my heart. It sounded too much like a goodbye. I tried to watch television, but after a few minutes I went back to check in on her and found her sleeping. After waiting another thirty minutes or so, I noticed that my foot had been, involuntarily, tapping the ground.

Anxious, I returned to the bedroom. Without turning on the light, I knew she had passed.

The room was filled with an overwhelming sense of peace. I hoped in that moment that the angel that she had seen on the moon had recently visited her and assured her that she was loved and would be taken care of.

Without warning, the palpable warm, tranquility vanished and secular reality punched me in the heart.

I had lost my mother.

From that point forward, I had hundreds of dreams of my mother. The first, and most precious to me, occurred just two days after her passing.

In the dream, we were standing in the kitchen of the house in which I spent the majority of my childhood. I asked her how she was doing. She replied that she was still having trouble regulating her blood pressure.

I somehow understood in the dream that she had still possessed aspects of her physical body after passing. My mom had high blood pressure the majority of her life and it had remained even after death. At least, in this dream.

We moved to the driveway where I helped my mother into a convertible car, with the top down. I then placed her cat in a carrier and secured it in the backseat. After handing her a plate of food, she began to drive off down the road.

I watched her drive off only to see her stop and return so that I could put the top up.

I had a convertible in my twenties and while she loved riding in it, the older adult in her would worry about the state of her hair in the whipping wind.

After putting the top up, she drove off and out of sight.

When I woke from this wonderful dream, I felt like I had taken care of her, even after she passed.

My mother had grown up near the water and often told me of the days that she would enjoy driving along the beaches with the convertible top down on her car.

During my childhood, we made frequent trips to the beach. Her favorite water spot was Ft. DeSoto Beach, which is where I spread her ashes.

I recall the drive to Ft. Desoto Beach after her memorial. I asked Selene for a pod of dolphins as a way of honoring my mother. I was more than grateful to see that when my brothers and I spread her ashes into the ocean, not one, but two pods of dolphins swam and jumped through the waves, just yards from us.

I still had one more thing to do and that was finding a home for my mother's cat.

Due to the canine hierarchy that ruled my home, I was unable to care for her feline companion. After weeks of searching for a home for her, I connected with an employee at my company, named Tonya. She told me that she managed a small cat rescue on her farm and would be willing to take my mom's former companion animal.

The cat was grumpy and, in my mother's estimation anyway, just *slightly* overweight. Regardless, it appeared that the feisty feline still had some life in front of her so I transferred custody.

A few weeks later, I was giving a presentation at a district meeting where Tonya was in attendance. During lunch, she happened to sit at my table with several other associates.

Without being asked, she blurts out, "Your mom's cat died."

I was dumfounded and just stared at her.

She continued. "I was sleeping on the couch the next day and as I woke up, someone whispered in my ear, 'Thank you for taking care of my cat.'"

Then, she got up and left the table. The other people, one by one, left as well until I was sitting alone trying to reconcile what Tonya had just told me. I felt like I had lost my mother all over again.

Somehow, I managed to conduct the remainder of my presentation, but I don't recall much of it.

That night, I dreamt of my mother. We were sitting on a front porch step and she was telling me that she was going to be reborn as a girl in Greensboro, North Carolina. After our chat, she said she had to leave. I watched her drive down a highway, and I feared for her safety on the busy roads. In the dream, I had a birds-eye view of the interstate and to the right of her car, I saw the same vast field with the colorful trees, running dogs and trail that I had seen in my own dream and during my visit to Greensboro.

I woke, knowing that my mother was going to be alright.

In this, and countless other dreams of my mother, she would never look at me. Her eyes would either be blurred out or she would not be facing me.

At first, I took this as concerning symbolism but then I recalled a phone call we received just hours after my mother passed. She had signed up to be an organ donor and they wanted permission to remove her eyes.

Once I remembered this, I would see her eyes in my dreams.

Chapter Eleven

It's early in 2015 and I'm only a few days away from turning 46 years old. While writing about my paranormal, metaphysical and spiritual experiences I have certainly relived all of them, to varying degrees.

In doing so, I am left to ponder their lingering effects on my life. Most significantly are the changes and growth that accompany an expanded awareness along with the pain of loss that I endure.

From my earliest experience, I became aware that I was in charge of my life. While we all surround ourselves with support mechanisms that we call family and friends, our journey is ours alone.

In my opinion, people aren't good or bad. They simply have a drive to survive and obtain their wants. Their decisions and actions to achieve their desires are what can blanket them in perceived lightness or darkness.

Everyone is responsible for their own lives and as much as they would love to help you out, they have to put themselves first. That's our world.

Sorry for the cynicism.

Sure, they can give you a ride to work or loan you money. When it comes to life decisions about where to work, who to date or what kind of person to be, most people will respond with, "That's up to you."

And, it is.

When I regressed into my past incarnations, I gained insight into my current personality traits as well as fears and insecurities. My reaction was twofold:

In one sense, I was relieved to understand where many of my quirks and fears came from.

As a child, I feared motorcycles and until my mid-twenties I could not sleep with covers on my legs. Once, I witnessed the horrific bike accident as Charles and the resulting loss of then-girlfriend, Julia, I released both issues.

Charles spent eleven years confined to a wheelchair. Prior to connecting to this lifetime, I would experience stomach pains any time I passed someone in a wheelchair. Sometimes, the pains would begin before I even saw the disabled individual.

Many of the lifetimes that I recalled held a similar theme of significant time alone. My turn as a young, enslaved, Irish girl was certainly sad and lonely. As a soldier in the French Army, I was alone when I enlisted and died amongst strangers after severe torture, in a subterranean prison.

I struggled in this life to become more social. While I have never been shy, I simply enjoyed being home alone with my interests.

The most difficult social settings were large, week-long conventions and meetings. It wasn't that I disliked the attendees or felt that the subject matter didn't warrant my attention. Oddly, I felt like my personal time was being taken from me.

Sharing a hotel room with a stranger along with early breakfasts and late dinners would leave no time for personal introspective, reading, writing, meditation or whatever I felt like doing. That personal freedom has always been very important to me.

In 7 Regressions, I wrote about my incarnations as Joey, a young boy with few friends who would lose himself in his imagination.

As a child, I had many friends but I did enjoy mid-afternoon "naps" where laid in bed lost myself in my imagination. I envisioned myself in various settings such as a general in the U.S. Calvary or as an astronaut flying into space to visit other planets.

Imagination is a vital component of writing and I am grateful that Joey's creative thought process surfaced in this particular lifetime.

Uncovering the carry-over predispositions of my previous lives gave me a sense of understanding. As a result, I became a lot less harsh on myself and more accepting of my behaviors.

Additionally, I gained a sense of control over who I was. Understanding why I preferred to be alone allowed me to accept it as something healthy rather than be concerned that I was a social outcast.

Most importantly, I found that I had the choice to change if I so desired. Often, I would tell myself to follow my "gut" and never go against its urging. Once I discovered that many of my instinctive feelings existed residually and were often an expired defense mechanism from a previous incarnation's trauma or drama, I was free to confidently deny them.

A great example can be found in my early attitude toward guns. For most of my life, I feared them. Furthermore, I didn't want to be around guns, hold them and by no means, ever shoot one.

Regressing to a simple lifetime as a young pioneer boy, I witnessed my father teaching me how to shoot a rifle. Sadly, the gun backfired and my face was left disfigured. Instead of comfort, my father blamed me for the accident. He felt, as a young man, I should inherently be adept at firing a gun. My father was embarrassed and

I was banished to barn work and rarely seen by anyone other than my family.

A hunter friend of mine offered to teach me how to shoot. At first, I declined while still clinging to my fear of not only the potential physical harm but that I would fail in both accuracy and technique.

Ever the patient teacher and boasting high quality firearms, he supplied me with protective gear and a safe environment in which to shoot.

Feeling safe with my goggles, ear plugs and modern shotgun, he talked me through the process of loading and finally shooting the gun. Thanks to his hands-on training and confidence in my ability, I successfully shot down the first two clays pulled at an outdoor range. Thus, I now "heart" guns.

Again, I took control of a fear and after identifying what was blocking my progress, I worked to move past it.

I see my fears as blocks and opportunities to grow. As a result, I feel a great sense of pride in my accomplishments as I work through them.

Unfortunately, I don't always succeed. To this day, I have a deeply ingrained fear of the dentist. My anxiety goes off the charts and actually neutralizes the numbing agents used in the offices.

The fear is so strong that I have to pay thousands to be put under anesthesia for general dentistry work to be completed. Basically, if they need to use the drill, they have to knock me out.

I have yet to access an incarnation where I suffered at the hand of some diabolical dentist and I don't recall any trauma from my childhood in this lifetime, either.

So far, all I can do is floss and brush religiously in an effort to deter any needed visits to the dentist.

Surely, hindsight has provided me with ample opportunity for growth which has enabled me to increase the quality of my life.

An even nicer gift that resulted from my metaphysical, paranormal and spiritual endeavors is my expanded awareness of the worlds around me.

If you are reading this book, then you most likely understand that there exist many worlds and in many dimensions. On occasion and if we are open to them, we can catch a glimpse.

Being aware of paranormal activity that suggests the presence of negative and intrusive spirits can, at the least, disrupt our lives. The entities can drain our energy, cause illness or even worse. An awareness of their potential interference allows us the chance to cleanse and banish them so that we operate out of a positive and nurturing environment.

Recently, I became very ill and suffered from attacks from an unseen force during astral travels and dream states. As I was lifting out of my body, someone or something grabbed both of my hands and held them behind my head. Unable to see the force behind me, I yelled repeatedly.

Finally, I awoke with my hands above my head and yelling at the top of my lungs.

Luckily, I was able to enlist the support of a Shaman friend who was able to remotely remove the spirit. Afterword, I followed his instructions of spraying holy water and sea salt around all entry points to the house.

My spiritual awareness allowed me to define and request the removal of the intruder. Without my understanding of the event, the experience could have been dismissed as a random nightmare and a dark force could continue to plague my home.

I can honestly say that my spiritual growth and paranormal awareness has helped me to understand and endure my lessons of loss.

I was comforted by my mother's encounter with the moon angel. My sensitivity allowed me to feel the warmth of peace and love that filled the room in which she passed. Also, years of dream interpretation experience enabled me to find solace in her passing as she said goodbye to me in the most amazing dream I have ever and will most likely, ever have.

My forty-five years of life in this incarnation have brought me to this point. I've written a series of short stories and this paranormal, true-experience book. I care for no less than two dogs at any given time and as I write this, I have four. I read a meme once that said, "Dogs are God's way of apologizing for relatives." That still makes me smile.

I'll continue to document my experiences and most likely, continue to write about them.

Most importantly, I'll go on living my life with both eyes open to everything, seen and unseen.

Epilogue

Thank you for reading my book and I appreciate your feedback by leaving a review on Amazon.com using this link:

https://www.amazon.com/review/create-review?ie=UTF8&asin=B00S38JVRO&channel=detail-glance&nodeID=133140011&ref_=cm_cr_dp_wrt_btm&store=digital-text#

7 Lessons-The 7 Novellas Series, based on the events that you just read, are available in a collection of 7 short stories via this link:

http://www.amazon.com/Lessons--Complete-Reincarnation-Paranormal-Experiences-ebook/dp/B00TQ7FSGO/ref=sr_1_3?ie=UTF8&qid=1425390694&sr=8-3&keywords=gare+allen

I highly recommend *Bones in the Basement* by Joni Mayhan which is also available on Amazon.com. The first three chapters are included here for your enjoyment. Enjoy!

BONES
IN THE BASEMENT

SURVIVING THE S.K. PIERCE HAUNTED VICTORIAN MANSION
Edwin Gonzalez & Lillian Otero's Story
JONI MAYHAN

Bones in the Basement
Surviving the S.K. Pierce Victorian Mansion

Edwin Gonzalez & Lillian Otero's Story

By

Joni Mayhan

Photo courtesy of Frank Grace (Trig Photography)

Chapter 1

The boy stared up at the creepy old house, feeling a lump grow in his throat.

The other kids wanted to break in and play a game of hide-and-seek. He wasn't sure he wanted to. Something about the house troubled him.

When he drove past it with his mother, he always glanced up at the dark windows, feeling like someone was watching him. Nobody had lived in the house for as long as he could remember, but everybody knew about it. It was the haunted Victorian mansion.

He went to school with a girl who used to live next door. She talked about seeing faces at the windows and lights blinking off and on all during the night. She told him that a man once burned to death in the house when he spontaneously combusted, and how his ghost still roamed the shadowed hallways. At the time, he swore he'd never go inside that scary old house, but here he was, all the same.

"Are you coming, Trevor?" one of the kids called.

He glanced around, noticing that he was the only one who hadn't crawled through the basement window yet. He swallowed the lump in his throat, wanting very badly to retreat to the safety of his home and watch an episode of *Scooby Doo* instead, but he couldn't figure how to do it without looking like a chicken.

He gave the house one more cautious glance and then climbed in after his friends.

I'll only stay for a little while. Then I'll tell them I have to go home for something.

They crept in through a basement window. The space was so dark, all he could see was the bobbing light from the flashlight ahead of him. Something brushed the back of his neck and he jolted with a gasp.

The other kids jumped too, but soon laughed as they realized what happened.

"What's the matter, Trevor? Afraid of a little spider's web?"

He took a deep breath to steady his nerves and tried to shake off the feeling that wouldn't leave him. They weren't supposed to be there. He could feel it in every cell of his body.

At the top of the stairs they found a doorway that led to the first floor. Trevor looked around, taking in the wooden floors and the furniture covered by sheets. It was exactly what he thought of when he imagined a haunted house. The only thing missing was the ghosts.

As they tiptoed through the old house, they began hearing strange sounds. At first, the sounds were subtle. They heard the creak of a floorboard in another room, which was followed by the echo of footsteps on the grand staircase.

One of the children started counting, so he scrambled up the grand staircase to the second floor to look for a hiding place.

The first room he came to had red walls. Something about the room made him feel uncomfortable, as if someone hid in the corner watching him. He gave the doorway a wide berth and studied the second room he came to.

It looked like it could have been a kid's bedroom. It was small and square, with two doorways and a strange looking closet. Something about the closet appealed to him. The door was short, as if it was made for a kid. As he stood in front of it, he heard the counting girl reach twenty.

"Ready or not, here I come," she announced.

He opened the closet door and scrambled in.

The darkness nearly closed in on him, so he cracked the door an inch and allowed a ribbon of light inside. He watched several kids run past the doorway, looking for a place to hide, as the counter made her way up the stairs.

"I see you, Jimmy!" she yelled.

Trevor held his breath, praying she didn't look in his direction. If she did, she'd probably find him in a second. It wasn't exactly the greatest hiding spot.

She continued past, and he let out his breath.

I made it.

He listened as the girl walked up the narrow staircase to the third floor, thinking that he'd just stay in the closet until all the other children were found. He heard the sound of more footsteps in the hallway. As he leaned forward to see who it was, something happened that would haunt him for the rest of his life. Hands grabbed onto his shoulders.

"Get out!" a voice whispered in his ear, before giving him a shove forward.

He stumbled out of the closet, a scream lodged deep in his throat.

As he rounded the doorway, he turned back in time to see a transparent boy grinning at him from the depths of the closet he'd just departed. He didn't stop running until he reached his own doorstep.

He wouldn't return to the house until years later, until his aunt Marion took him on a tour.

Edwin and Lillian in 2013

Chapter 2

Edwin's stomach twisted into knots as they drove to look at a Victorian mansion in Gardner. He wasn't sure why they were driving so far to look at a house. They already had a house, and he was perfectly happy where they were, but once Lillian caught wind of the mansion, there was no resisting her. Lillian loved Victorians like some women loved fine jewelry.

He glanced at her sitting in the passenger seat, her long black hair pulled into a high, sleek ponytail. She wore heavy silver earrings that swung back and forth as her head bobbed to the beat of the music. Her happiness was nearly contagious. He couldn't help smiling at her, causing some of his uneasiness to slough away.

It was hard to believe they'd been together for over twenty years. They met at the bindery factory where they both worked at the time. He was blown away the first time he saw her walking across the parking lot, her dark hair dancing around her face as she laughed. He was enamored in an instant, something he still felt years later. There was nothing he wouldn't do for her.

Their happily-ever-after led them to an ordinary existence in Dorchester, a Boston neighborhood, where they shared a triple-decker with Lillian's mother and sister. Life was comfortable, if not predictable, with the fixtures of friends and family surrounding them like a safety net. The days passed by with a steady hum, the highs and lows too minimal to notice. Days were spent working at their respective jobs, while weekends were consumed by daytrips to antique stores and to local restaurants, or doing repairs around the house. Everything changed when Lillian's sister showed her a real estate listing for a Victorian mansion. Their lives were promptly fractured into a thousand pieces. Nothing would ever be comfortable or predictable again.

Edwin wasn't sure what to make of Lillian's sudden need to see the house.

It was more than just a passing fancy or a decision made after seeing something alluring and wanting a closer look. It was more of an obsession, a dire need as magnetic as the pull of addiction. Once she saw the listing, she had to go there. There was no other option.

It troubled Edwin on several levels. Lillian was usually so fastidious. She wasn't reckless or prone to impulse. She had an agenda, and she usually stuck with it. It was one of the things he loved most about her. She was consistent. She made lists and schedules; she thought things out to the last detail before she reacted. He knew what to expect of her, and it gave him a great sense of comfort. Her suggesting they go look at a house sixty miles out of town was very much out of character for her. At first, he blamed it on her passion for Victorians.

Lillian had loved Victorians since she was a little girl. She used to live down the street from a beautiful Victorian. She walked past it every day on her way to school, swearing that one day she'd have a house just like it. The dream stayed with her through her adulthood. He often caught her scrolling through the real estate listings, daydreaming about owning one, but it had never advanced to a point where they actually got in the car to go look at one.

By the way she described it, the house they were driving to sounded similar to the house of her childhood dreams. The Second Empire Victorian mansion was over six-thousand square feet in size, and had twenty-six rooms, including a tower that rose above the house, providing sweeping views of South Gardner. According to the realtor, the house had been vacant for the past two years as the owner tried to find a buyer. Every deal that came through for the house mysteriously fell apart. It was as if the house was waiting for the right owner.

"Are you excited?" Edwin asked, reaching over to hold Lillian's hand.

She turned, her lips curving into a broad smile that lit up her entire face. "I'm beyond excited. Just imagine living in our own Victorian," she said, staring wistfully off into space.

Edwin wished he could be half as excited.

Part of his anxiety was based in reality. Victorians were known to be money pits. An old house would require a lot of upkeep, something he wasn't sure they could handle both physically and financially. He imagined the long hours and the added expenses, and it was enough to make him sigh. The other reason was the uneasy feeling in his gut.

Something just wasn't right about that house.

He knew it from the minute he called the realtor to request a viewing. The woman had been very strange about it. She asked him at least three times if he was sure he wanted to see *that* house.

And then there was the dream.

He'd barely fallen asleep the night before, when he found himself in the middle of the strangest dream.

In the dream, he found himself drifting through the massive front door of a Victorian mansion. It was as though he didn't have feet or legs. He just floated along like a ghost on the wind. He looked up to see a bright chandelier shining above him, the light casting dark whimsical shadows into the corners of the room. To his right, he heard the melodic sound of music.

It was soft and enchanting, the kind of music people listened to at the turn of the century. The house had a glorious feeling to it, as if people were at the highest peak of their lives, thoroughly enjoying all the wealth and splendor it offered them. It was like a vintage snapshot in time, encapsulating the souls who refused to relinquish the moment. He felt himself traveling towards a set of white doors towards the source of the music, unable and unwilling to stop.

The doors swung open as he approached them, and he found himself in the midst of a large social gathering.

People crowded inside the parlor room, dressed in early Victorian finery. Ice cubes clinked in glasses as drinks were served, and the hum of conversation filled the air. Women with bright smiles talked to one another, while dapper men shared confidences over a glass of finely-aged brandy. The room smelled of perfume and pipe smoke, which caught the light as it clouded the air.

No one seemed to notice him as he silently wafted into the room.

He floated among them as if he were invisible.

They smiled and talked to one another, their voices momentarily rising above the lilting sound of the music. As Edwin glided further into the depths, the crowd parted and he became aware of a man sitting in the middle of the room.

Unlike the others, the man was watching him. He was dressed all in black with a debonair mustache that curled upwards at the ends. With his straight carriage and direct gaze, he presented himself as the master of the house. He nodded at Edwin as if welcoming him to the party, a slight knowing smile curving the corners of his lips. And with that, Edwin woke up, feeling disoriented like he just time traveled back from a bygone era.

Lillian squeezed his hand and he glanced back at her, coming back to reality from his daydream. She was still smiling.

"We really need something good to happen to us," she told him.

He sighed again.

It was true. Their dog Casper passed away several months ago, and it was a devastating blow for both of them. Their dogs were like family members, and losing one left a large hole in their lives. Edwin hadn't seen Lillian smile so broadly since Casper's death. Maybe this would be a good thing for them both.

He tried to clear his mind of the nagging feelings so he could enjoy the moment.

Lillian was right. They needed something good to happen to them.

Photographic rendition of Edwin's dream

CHAPTER 3

Bill Wallace sat across the street from the Victorian, nursing a beer at the South Gardner Hotel. Voices and music buzzed around him, but he hardly noticed. His eyes trained through the milky window as he stared at the golden-yellow mansion on the corner.

Something was changing in that house, and he didn't like it.

Bill looked like a cross between Santa Claus and Albert Einstein. With his full white beard and wild hair, he came across as an eccentric sort at first, but there was an intelligence and warmth in his eyes that made people reconsider their first impression.

He always knew he was different. Routine things didn't interest him. He always found himself drawn to the peculiar side of life, the intricacies and the elements that most people never considered. Life was more than what it seemed. He knew this on an empathic, psychic level. While he never called himself a psychic medium, his talents as an empathic medium were undeniable.

His family was known to have the gift of psychic insight. His father used to spend countless hours trying to surprise Bill's grandmother with a visit, but no matter when they showed up at her house, she was ready for them, often with a meal on the table. Bill's own abilities didn't surface until after he died during triple bypass surgery and was successfully resuscitated. When he woke up, he wasn't the same person.

He could talk to ghosts.

Bill could feel the spirits calling to him as he walked the streets of Gardner. He would look up at the side of the buildings, sometimes seeing an apparition standing there, silently watching him. The Victorian Mansion had been pulling at him for several years.

When most people drove past the house, they looked up at the dark windows and wondered if someone was looking back at them. Bill didn't have to wonder. He knew they were there.

The spirit of a young woman named Mattie had been there since the late 1800's. Petite, with long dark hair that she wore in a bun, she once cared for the Pierce children. Bill saw her as a kind person with a charitable heart, but not someone who tolerated nonsense. Chores were scheduled at specific times, and the children were taught to behave. Even though she was long dead, she remained the protector of the house, keeping it safe from trespassers and ensuring the other resident ghosts behaved themselves.

He became aware of her as he drove past the house on Union Street. He heard the sounds of her in his head, singing a folk song he had never heard before. At the time, he discounted the sound as a consequence from his near-death experience, but after a while he couldn't deny it. She was reaching out to him.

She was calling to him again as he sat across the street, asking for his help.

Unfortunately, Bill had no way of getting inside the house. It had been vacant for two years since the previous owners left. Breaking and entering wasn't something he was willing to do.

"Sorry, Mattie. No can do," he whispered under his breath.

He looked at the house, wondering what was transpiring behind those dark and dingy windows. Whatever it was, it wasn't good.

Bill's relationship with the mansion started in 2000.

He and his friend Mike were sitting on the hood of his car at the pizza shop across the street, waiting for their order. It was late August and the night was thick with humidity and mosquitoes. Mike was talking about the religious training he was undergoing to become a minister, but Bill hardly heard a word he said. All he could do was stare at the house across the street.

He could feel Mattie lingering near a second floor window, watching him.

Bill was pulled from his daydream when a man burst out of the Victorian mansion and started walking towards them. Bill was immediately captivated by the sight.

The tall, dark-haired man was dressed in a long black coat and had a decided air of confidence to him. Bill laughed when he saw him because, for all the world, he reminded him of Gomez Addams walking out of his creepy haunted house. He was surprised when the man crossed the street and headed towards the pizza shop.

The minute the man approached them, the two made eye contact. Bill, being the jovial type, began humming the theme song to *The Addams Family*. The man seemed taken back for a moment, but recovered after a minute. The two then introduced themselves.

"Mark Veau," the man said, giving Bill a firm handshake. Bill nodded and introduced himself as well, finding himself instantly drawn to Mark's unique character.

The fact that he owned such a magnificent house only added to the allure.

"That's a beautiful house," Bill told him, looking over Mark's shoulder at the yellow mansion. It was as though he couldn't look away for long before his gaze was pulled back to those spellbinding windows.

"Would you like to see it?" Mark asked.

Bill nearly lunged for the door. "Very much so," he said, almost forgetting about his friend in his eagerness to see the house.

They came through the door, and Bill felt the outside world melt away. All he could think about was getting upstairs to see Mattie. Mark introduced him to his fiancée Suzanne, but he barely noticed. His gaze was pulled to the staircase.

As they passed the wall to his right, Bill felt a sizzle run up the side of his body. He stopped and looked at his arm. Every hair was standing on end. It was as if the house had an electrical current running right through it. He could feel it buzzing in the air like a pulse.

He found himself walking towards the stairs. He knew it was odd, not waiting for Mark to lead the tour, but there was something about the upstairs that he had to see. It was where Mattie waited. Being so deliciously close was more than he could handle. He needed to see her now.

Even though he never saw the inside the house before, he instinctively knew the layout. He walked up the servant's staircase to the second floor, then made his way down the long hallway.

The space was different than it was in the 1880's when Mattie lived there. The walk-in closet off the master bedroom was once a small sewing room. She liked to sit here and crochet doilies out of bits of string that she found on packages.

The doorway that once connected the room to the second floor landing had been plastered over many years ago, turning it into a closet. Mattie still spent ample amounts of time there, preferring the quietness of the room to the more congested areas of the house. It was where she went to collect her thoughts.

Mattie.

The minute she noticed him, she reached out to him with her mind. She seemed happy to see him, pleased to finally find someone who could communicate with her. She told him many things, the words nearly tumbling out too fast for comprehension. It was as though she'd kept them bottled up for decades and the pressure of releasing them was just too much for her to handle.

"Bill?" Mark said, touching his arm. "Are you okay?"

Bill snapped out of it long enough to explain. "Every time I drive by, she calls to me. She likes it here," he said.

Mark gave him a curious glance. "Are you talking about Mattie Cornwell? The nanny?" he asked.

Bill was surprised that Mark knew about Mattie. "You know about her?"

Mark smiled. "Several weeks after we moved in, our contractor told us the house was haunted and asked if he could bring in his two nieces who were mediums. They told me about her," he said with an incredulous tone. "How do you know about her?"

Bill told Mark about his gift, never worrying that the other man would think he was crazy. There seemed to be an instant understanding between the two of them that the friendship would never be what other people considered normal. Bill was just as colorful as Mark.

"She takes care of the house. She always has," he told Mark. "This house sat empty for over twenty years before you bought it. Do you ever wonder how this house made it through the years of being abandoned without suffering immense damage?" he asked.

Mark looked at him inquisitively. "What do you mean?"

Bill pointed to the pristine woodwork that framed every window, doorway, floor, and ceiling. "You would think after twenty years of sitting empty with people sneaking in here day and night, someone would have carved their initials into the woodwork, or even burned one of the doors for warmth. Mattie's the reason why they didn't."

Mark nodded and then shared a story of his own. "I've had several psychics tell me the same thing. There's even a police report to prove it. Back in the seventies, Mattie chased two guys out of here," Mark said.

"Really?"

Mark smiled. "Yeah, they were just thugs. They were were up to no good. They broke into the house, thinking they were going to steal something, but they got the crap scared out of them instead. Somebody called the police because one of the guys ended up outside on the ground in a fetal position blubbering about being chased out of the house. Apparently, the cops searched the house and didn't find anyone inside. They told the guy on the sidewalk that he must have imagined it. There was nobody in the house. The guy looked up at them from the sidewalk and stated, 'I said we were chased out of the house. I didn't say it was somebody,'" Mark finished with a smile.

He went on to share what he knew about Mattie Cornwell.

She was born in 1859 in Nova Scotia, Canada. She was twenty-one when she came to work for the Pierce family as a servant in the house. Her primary focus was caring for the Pierce children. She was firm but loving with the children, keeping them mindful of their manners and helping them grow into the influential men they would one day become.

Later research would show that Mattie died at the young age of twenty-five from an acute inflammation of the hip just two years after getting married. Her tragedy would be just one among many at the Victorian mansion. It was as if the house collected them, like some people collected old coins.

Bill opened his mouth to respond, but was suddenly overwhelmed by a tightening in his chest. He slumped back against the wall as the world faded around the edges.

"Are you okay?" Mark asked with concern. "Do you need me to call an ambulance?"

Bill took a few breaths before he answered. Although he felt weak, he was fairly certain he wasn't having another heart attack. It was something else altogether. It was the house. It was getting to him. "No. I'm fine," he finally managed to say. "Just let me catch my breath for a second."

After a few minutes, he began to feel better, but the sensation was momentary. Visions began to flood his mind. He could barely get the words out.

"Mattie doesn't like your dog," he told Mark. "They had dogs at the mansion, but they were never allowed to run loose around the house. It bothers her because the master of the house would have never allowed it."

Mark seemed taken back. "How do you know I have a dog?" he asked.

Bill stared down at the floor. "Because I can see him in the basement. He's a big black fluffy dog," he said. It was as though he could see straight through the floors.

Mark gave him a dubious look. "That's unreal," he said. "You can really see that?"

Bill wasn't finished with his visions. "There's something in the house that Mattie doesn't like. You need to find it and get it out," he said.

He began to describe an area of the basement, an area he had never seen. "It's in a room with a fieldstone foundation near a set of stairs. It's flat. It might be a document, or a piece of paper, but you'll know it when you see it."

After Bill left, Mark and his wife searched the basement until they found the item Bill had described. It was a canning jar with Nazi swastikas drawn on the label. It was tucked into a bookcase along the backside of the wall behind the servant's staircase. The moment Mark moved the jar across the threshold of the property, a sudden gust of wind caught the label and whisked it away. They never found out who drew the swastikas on the label or why Mattie was so offended by them, but it seemed to appease her nonetheless.

Unfortunately, Mark and Suzanne's marriage only lasted until 2006. When they divorced, the house went back on the market. It took two years before they accepted a solid bid, years that left Bill on the outside looking in again.

Something in the house was changing.

A plan was set into motion and nothing would stop it until it reached the end.

If you enjoyed this preview of Bones in the Basement, please find it on Amazon.com or Barnesandnoble.com in both EBook or paperback.

http://www.amazon.com/Bones-Basement-Surviving-Victorian-Gonzalez-ebook/dp/B00KQQRH72/ref=sr_1_3?ie=UTF8&qid=1418882752&sr=8-3&keywords=joni+mayhan